History in the Present Tense

History in the Present Tense

ENGAGING STUDENTS THROUGH INQUIRY AND ACTION

DOUGLAS SELWYN AND JAN MAHER

HEINEMANN
Portsmouth, NH

907.1
S469h
2003

Heinemann
A division of Reed Elsevier Inc.
361 Hanover Street
Portsmouth, NH 03801–3912
www.heinemann.com

Offices and agents throughout the world

© 2003 by Douglas Selwyn and Jan Maher

Library of Congress Cataloging-in-Publication Data
Selwyn, Douglas, 1949–
     History in the present tense : engaging students through inquiry and action /
     Douglas Selwyn and Jan Maher.
         p.   cm.
     Includes bibliographical references.
     ISBN 0-325-00570-2 (alk. paper)
     1. Social sciences—Problems, exercises, etc. 2. Social sciences—Study and teaching—
Activity programs.   I. Maher, Jan.   II. Title.

H62.3.S457   2003
907'.1—dc21   2003009955

Editor: Danny Miller
Production editor: Sonja S. Chapman
Cover design: Catherine Hawkes, Cat & Mouse
Cover photo: Judi Slepyan
Compositor: David Stirling, Black Dog Graphics
Manufacturing: Steve Bernier

Printed in the United States of America on acid-free paper
07   06   05   04   03   VP   1   2   3   4   5

Contents

Preface

History, despite its wrenching pain,

cannot be unlived,

and if faced with courage,

need not be lived again.

—Maya Angelou

Millions of people have a story to tell of September 11, 2001. For most of us in the United States, it starts with waking up on an otherwise normal September morning to the horrific images of the World Trade Center in flames. The news of terrorist attacks on this symbol of our system, followed by the news of the attack on the Pentagon, brought us the realization that a wrenching, painful history was in the making, and that we were right in the middle of it. This was so even if we had little or no sense of where that history was coming from, or why we were part of it.

An event of this awful magnitude sets us going in many directions at once. We are hungry for answers. We want to understand. But we also hunger for simplicity. We want it to be easy to understand. We long for yesterday, fear for tomorrow, want peace, want revenge. We need, indeed our lives depend on, the ability to know both the causes of such an event and the potential consequences of our responses.

We need the full range of social studies—understanding of self;

understanding of others; awareness of political, economic, cultural and religious issues among groups of people; understanding of physical geography; understanding of historical antecedents; and comprehension of why terrorism doesn't respect national boundaries any more than global free trade does. In short, we need to know where this story really started, and where it might really go so that we can, as poet Maya Angelou says, face it with courage and hope that we can avert repeating its horrors.

But the pain of September 11 comes at a time when the social studies themselves are under attack. Under pressure for their students to perform well on standardized tests of reading, writing, and mathematics, some elementary schools have entirely eliminated social studies from their curriculum. In states where social studies are tested as part of the high-stakes standardized test mania, programs of proven quality and recognized merit are giving way to a focus solely on preparation for these tests, many of which confront students with questions on a dizzying array of unrelated details and gross generalities.

We must resist this trend. The survival of our democracy is dependent on an informed citizenry, able to make reasoned decisions based on critical thinking. The courage that the poet calls for must be grounded in knowledge—of ourselves and of others; of the historical, geographic, political, and economic forces that shape our world; and of our democratic values. An informed citizenry must be grounded in essential social studies skills: the ability to distinguish opinion from fact, to recognize cause and effect, to work as part of a group toward a common goal. The National Council for the Social Studies has articulated what must be our goal—to help young people develop the ability to make informed and reasoned decisions for the public good as citizens of a culturally diverse, democratic society in an interdependent world.

This book is written in the hope of making a contribution to that effort.

—Douglas Selwyn and
Jan Maher
SelwynMaher@aol.com

Acknowledgments

We are most grateful for the help we have received from educators and students around the country, and we would like to thank them.

Connie Coffman, Wendy Ewbank, Sarah Heller McFarlane, Adora Callas and the Summit trio of Jo Cripps, Kristin Nichols, and Gail Powers took portions of our book for test drives with their students, and offered wise and tactful observations and council about how we could strengthen the work. We thank them for their patience, their enthusiasm, their generosity, and their wisdom.

Bobby Morrison, Victoria Bernstein, and Faith Beatty worked with Jan on a number of projects where students literally took center stage. We are thankful for Faith's assistance, too, in helping us find student work samples from some of those projects.

Laura Wendling, professor of education at California State University at San Marcos, provided resources for conducting oral histories. John Gaines provided photography resources.

It's hard to know what to say about Don Fels. He is an extraordinary artist and teacher who is both an inspiration and a whirlwind. We developed the trading stories lesson together, though it is fully based on his work as an artist/researcher. It's what he does all of the time. He's doing it at this very moment!

Steve Goldenberg is an extraordinary teacher who continues to keep his eyes on the prize. The prize is nurturing and supporting his students to follow their hearts and minds to learn about the world.

Tina and Mike Dawson provided laptops, excursions out into the world, and long talks about the nature of things, and the things of nature.

Judi Slepyan, the photography wizard who graced the pages of *Social*

Studies at the Center (Heinemann 2000), was Doug's coconspirator in the photography project described in these pages, and provided expertise, more expertise, and countless hours in service to that project. We thank her again for the use of one of her magnificent photographs, and for her dedication to supporting education. And we thank her for the cover photo. Josh Ackerman was our digital photographer; we thank him for always being willing to take yet another set of pictures of students and their work.

We thank our colleagues at Antioch University in Seattle and Heritage College, who share a vision of education and work unstintingly to make it happen.

We thank many other teachers and friends who so generously shared their own ideas, observations, and time, including Mike Sullivan, Rosalie Ramono, Barbara Cemeno, Kathy Purcell, Rebecca Timson, Christie McLean-Kesler, Joanne DuFour, Carole Williams, Carol Reed, Maeve Doolittle, Gail Mitchell, Jim Gibson, Nikki Nojima Louis, Julie Weston, Elizabeth Zumwalt, Rebecca Hughes, Paul Loeb, Adrian Flynn, Walter Parker, all the members of Puget Sound Rethinking Schools and of the Washington State Council for the Social Studies. We thank online friends and acquaintances whose discussions of teaching and learning always help us to hone our own ideas. And Puget Sound Writing Project for supporting teachers as writers.

Our parents, James T. Maher, Jr., Allen Lang, Ruth Lang, William Selwyn, and Jean Selwyn, who always encouraged questions, and always answered them with "Let's find out." Our sisters, Diana Maher, Wendy Valentino, and Laurie Selwyn who shared the journeys. Our now adult children, Noah, Josh, and Rachelle Ackerman, whose curiosity, compassion, and stubborn individuality continue to delight us. Thank you.

And then there are our students. There are not enough words to express our appreciation and gratitude for the teacher education students at Antioch University, Heritage College, Western Washington University, and the University of Washington with whom we have worked and with whom we continue to work. It can be very challenging to teach in public education these days. That students of such passion, skill, hope, and promise are entering a profession that needs them so badly brings light and hope to us.

To the public school students with whom we have worked, at Beacon Hill, Summit K–12, Cleveland High School, Roosevelt High School, Nathan Hale High School, NOVA and elsewhere: You are truly why we do what we do. Keep asking your questions, keep following your dreams and your hearts, and stay active and involved. We need you.

We, of course, thank Danny Miller for his skills, enthusiasm, patience, tact, and wise counsel as editor of this book; Sonja Chapman who served us well as our production editor; and, as always, the good folks at Heinemann who have offered skilled, effective support throughout the process.

Introduction: The Politics of Pronouns

Consider the pronoun, a modest part of speech too shy to be named formally or frontally. Lacking an identity of its own, the pronoun only stands in for someone or something else. Pronouns are so quiet, so common, and so seemingly familiar that we don't quite notice them. But pronouns are sly as well as shy. They often carry a very strong message about who *we* are and how *we* see the world. And they carry challenging questions: Are *you* part of *us*? Does *we* include *me*? When *we*, the people, are working for the common good, does that common good include *me*? Or *you*?

The quiet threat and danger in pronouns is the assumed agreements that underlie their usage. One assumed agreement is that the user can clearly define who falls into the category of the pronoun. Sometimes it's easy. "*We* went skiing yesterday"—I know precisely to whom I am referring, and the listener or reader is clear about this. Sometimes it's not so clear or obvious, as in: "*They* don't value life the way *we* do." *They* are bad guys; *we* are good guys.

This suggests a second assumed agreement. The speaker or writer using these constructs assumes and implies that speaker and listener (writer and reader) share (or should share) the same frame of reference and value system such that the meaning of the pronoun is clearly the same to each. During the Vietnam era, *we* were presumably Americans, probably Christians, and good; *they* were North Vietnamese/Viet Cong, probably non-Christians, probably communists, and bad. More recently, *they* are Arabs, most certainly Muslims. When someone says, "It's the way we do things around here," there is a clear message implied that if *you* want to be part of *we*, you'd better do things that way too.

A third assumed agreement is that those grouped within *we* are grouped accurately and absolutely by the speaker or writer according to a common, significant trait. There are no subtle gradations or exceptions allowed for when categorizing people as *we* or *they, us* or *them*. Pronouns make it very difficult to be less than absolute and categorical, to spin less than a very wide web. You are either with *us* or against *us*.

Whose World-Class City Is This?

I (Doug, self-referential to a fault) began to think about the role that pronouns play in our lives when business and political leaders in Seattle began to lobby citizens of the Puget Sound area to use taxpayer dollars to fund the building of a privately owned baseball stadium. The then lowly Mariners were playing in a concrete mausoleum called the Kingdome. It was an engineering marvel, tons and tons of concrete constructed to outlast us all. Solidly built, utilitarian, no art or pretense to it. Aesthetics? Nah. But it functioned; it kept the rain out (mostly), kept the roof on (mostly), and was relatively cheap. It took a great deal of explosives to implode because it was so resolutely what it was.

But, it was not sexy; it did not have luxury boxes; it did not have open air or sunset views, or a winning baseball team playing in it. It was, in short, not a world-class stadium. And the political and business leaders of the Puget Sound region told the region's citizens, who would have to vote approval for a new stadium, that *we* in the region deserved to have a world-class stadium in a world-class city. It was time for *us* to step up to the plate and get what *we* deserved.

But who was the *we*? Few of the people I asked felt included in that pronoun. Not school teachers, not social workers, not students, not working-class folks. A very small percentage of the people I spoke with in the neighborhood in which the new stadium would be built considered themselves part of that particular *we*. Many of those living in the neighborhood would be forced to move their businesses or residences so that the stadium could be constructed. None of the street folks who populated the adjacent Pioneer Square area, who would be forced out by the *upgrade* to world-class status, seemed to feel that *they* were part of the *we*. The homeless in the nearby downtown region didn't seem very concerned about whether the city in which they were homeless was world class or not. *We* did not seem likely to include *them*.

It began to seem like the *we* who were going to enjoy the status that goes with being a world-class city didn't actually live in it. *We* lived in the suburbs, across the lake, or a ferry-ride away to the west. Or perhaps in some entirely other city or state, drawn as a moth to flame by the potential profits in a new world-class stadium in the newly designated world-class city.

By the end of 1995, some public perceptions and energies had shifted. There was a stunning turn of events: The perpetually lowly Seattle Mariners baseball team had begun to win. Perennial doormats of the American League West, *our* local heroes came from very far back in the pack and eventually, on the day the season ended, won the Western Division playoffs, and the right to face the dreaded Damn Yankees of song and story. And, impossibly, the Mariners won. *We* won! *Our* team beat *their* team. Local media trumpeted the results on an hourly basis. Conversations around town centered on how *we* did last night. *Our* heroes were elevated to one-name or nickname celebrity status. Junior, Randy, A-Rod, Lou. Our guys. We're number one.

But, again, there was something wrong with the picture. Our team? Our guys? Interesting concept. The players were essentially arms, legs, gloves, and bats for hire, overpaid workers who happened to be employed by the Seattle branch of the baseball industry during that season. And the four just mentioned are now *their* guys—all playing for or managing other teams in other cities. The owners of the team actually also own Nintendo; *our* Mariners are actually part of a Japanese conglomerate.

Owners around the country echoed the threat made in Seattle: Build us a stadium or we will leave, a sort of musical chairs quick-step that featured privatized profits and socialized expenses and losses. We (the owners) make money, while we (the taxpayers) pay the expenses. Now, which *we* were number one? If *our* team left, *we* would be here in a baseball-less, world-classless city, while *our* team became somebody else's home team, and *our* guys would be *their* guys. The players would, of course, be paid millions either way. The voters of King County, by a slim margin, voted against raising taxes to build *them* a stadium. And yet the new stadium stands. *Our* state legislature decided that the voters of King County were surely mistaken and overrode the decision.

"We're Number One"—but who are we? What does that mean? *We* didn't play. *We* didn't make millions. Most of us didn't even go to the games, or paid dearly to do so if we did. It is curious. Our taxes went up to pay for the stadium. Our ticket prices went up to pay for the stadium and for our players' contracts. Our rents went up in and around the newly world-class neighborhood surrounding the world-class stadium, so much so that some of us could no longer afford to maintain our houses, apartments, or businesses. Our traffic is worse, our parking problems are multiplied, and the stadium was built despite the fact that *we* voted against it. . . . They own it.

Whose Country Is This?

It is not a trivial question. When the topic turns to the more obviously polit-ical arena the pronouns take on much more observable heat. *We* have learned that referring to the human race as men is leaving out half of it. And it's not enough to say, "Well, you know what I meant." It was more accurate than perhaps intended to have our famous founding document note that "all men are created equal." Of course, it wasn't all that accurate either, as Native American, African American, or non-land-owning European Americans knew all too well. Who were, who are, "*We*, the People?"

The United States is technically a democratic republic, but there are millions of citizens who cannot vote, who have no say in what happens to us in *our* lives. Other people decide and tell us what we will do, what we can do, or what will happen to *us* if we don't do. For years, young men could be arrested for refusing to fight in wars that leaders they could not vote for commanded them to fight in. Were they included in this notion of democracy, or a democratic republic?

When *we* have studied *our* history—the history of the United States—who have *we* studied and from whose point of view? Accounts of Columbus, through the early 1990s, presented a very one-sided picture of the "discovery of America." I (and virtually every other student in the United States) was taught that a European Christian, with bravery and skill, came to an uncivi-lized, primitive, and decidedly un-Christian land and claimed it (and all the people on it) for God and for his employer. He was widely recognized as a hero and the date of his landing was celebrated as a national holiday. This was defined as the moment when *our* history as a civilized nation began. The native people who greeted Columbus when his boat touched sand have been relegated for five hundred years to bit players in this European American version of who *we* are. They were cast as godless savages who had finally been discovered, been kissed awake by the explorer prince, who crossed the great water, carrying civilization with him.

Stories challenging this Euro-centered version of national history were kept to the fringes until the virtual eve of the five hundredth anniversary of the landing. Finally, stories that brought another point of view were added to *our* history. These stories helped *us* realize that Native Americans do not view Columbus as a hero; they view his coming not so much as a discovery as an invasion. *Our* story has grown a bit larger, a bit more complex, though the process has not been without controversy. *We* don't always welcome change.

When I look to the students in many of our public schools, I have a hard time finding their stories within the textbook histories of *our* country. When the students and I studied the American Revolution, we had a conversation about the issue of voting and representation, issues of no small importance to the founders. There was only one person in our classroom who would have been able to vote in our democracy at the time of *our* revolution, and that was me. That's true even assuming that the students would have been of voting age and from families that owned their own homes (other factors in the voting rights question). None of the girls would have been permitted to vote. None of the Native American students; none of the African American students; none of the students of Chinese, Japanese, Filipino, Korean, Latino/a, Vietnamese, Laotian, or other heritage. I was the only European American male in the room. So *whose* democracy was this?

Even the families of most European American students are rarely featured. This country doesn't really belong to them either, although there are more photos in the books of people who look like them. When students learn that they don't really belong to *our* story, I wonder what message that carries, what damage that does.

The students and I went through the textbooks supplied by the district and noted the topics; the pictures; the issues; and the points of view expressed in chapter titles, in captions, in maps and charts, and in what is included or excluded. Chapters titled Discovery, Westward Expansion, The Founding of the Nation, Manifest Destiny, Growth and Expansion, The Growing Nation, Exploring the Americas, make it very clear whose story is being told, who is outside or insignificant, or is on the *wrong* side of that story. There is a definite point of view, a frame of reference that is unstated but clear—*we* know who we are, and who we are not.

Whose World Is This?

The scene is just as problematic when the class is World History. Many public schools in the United States offer world history courses that barely give lip service to Central or South America, and scarcely mention Canada. The countries of Turkey, Iran, Iraq, and Egypt have ancient histories, disconnected sometimes even in name from their contemporary forms. The region they occupy is actually defined by where it isn't (the Middle East being midway between Europe and the Far East). Asia and China have ancient histories as well, then disappear. Places reappear when they become colonies, or fight wars with the West. Contemporary Afghanistan will undoubtedly make it into the next round of publications as the country that harbored America's Most Wanted, and Iraq has reemerged as a U.S.-declared threat to the security of the world. Students never get any sense of who the people of Iraq, Afghanistan, Russia, Burkina Faso, or Guatemala, or Argentina, or Vietnam are on their own terms, through their own eyes. World history is a history of a few places of the world as defined by a Western point of view.

This self-centered approach is probably the rule rather than the exception in educational systems around the world. There is a limited amount of time, resources, and expertise, and the task of really learning about people on their own terms rarely is taken on in our neighborhoods, much less in reference to those who live outside our national boundaries, across the world from us. Throughout history, peoples have tended to refer to themselves as *the people* and the rest of the world in lesser terms *(barbarians, heathens, savages, infidels)*. But recent events have made it very clear that this approach to learning about the world is woefully inadequate.

Mr. Hirata, an Aikido teacher in Seattle, used to say that we are each at the center of the Universe. *I* (said he) am at the center, and so are each of *you. We* are each at the center and have both rights and responsibilities as such. No one is more at the center than is anyone else.

We (Doug, Jan, and all the rest of us) find ourselves now, at the beginning of the twenty-first century, in a world with more than six billion *centers*. It is urgently important that we learn both to find ourselves at the center and to be able to understand the point of view of others at their *own* centers. For our own democracy to survive and flourish, "We, the People" of the United States must expand to truly encompass *all* the people who live within our borders. And "We, the People" of this earth must learn to live together on this fragile planet to secure our future. This is the province of social studies; this is our responsibility as social studies educators. As the National Council for the Social Studies states: "The primary purpose of social studies is to help young people develop the ability to make informed and reasoned decisions for the public good as citizens of a culturally diverse, democratic society in an interdependent world" (1994, vii).

So, if we are classroom teachers, we have a crucial choice to make. We are assigned classes to teach, with a specific content, often linked to a (usually) preselected textbook. We can retreat into that book, and teach that predetermined content that places few of our students at the center of anything. Or, we can recognize the opportunity to help our students connect with their world. We can support them to connect their own lives with the events recorded in history books and with events happening at this moment. We can support them to see themselves as actors in an immediate context connected to the past and the future, and to help them to realize that the choices they and their peers make will be what we read about in history books in the future.

This doesn't mean throwing out the textbook; however, it does mean using it as a reference and scaffold rather than as the final word. It means knowing where to find other resources that bring richness, diversity, complexity, immediacy, and context to the course of study.

What we offer in this book are templates for a number of projects that lend themselves naturally to giving students opportunities to learn important social studies content and skills by engaging in student-centered meaningful, memorable activities. Each unit begins in the here and now, using students' present concerns and circumstances as a springboard for exploring curricula. Any of these projects can be undertaken essentially as we describe them, but each can also be shaped and adapted to various grade levels, course content, and communities. We give examples of how these projects look at various grade levels, including preservice teacher education. We also give examples of how, beginning in the present and centering on student interests, a teacher can connect thematically to the important content of any social studies subject.

In his book *Media Unlimited* (2002), Todd Gitlin retells an old parable. Gitlin's version features a crossing guard and a truckdriver at the Mexican border. The truckdriver passes through the border checkpoint weekly, if not monthly; the border guard, convinced that he is smuggling something, searches his trucks each time and finds nothing. On the day the border guard is to retire, he says to the truckdriver that he (the border guard) knows that he (the truckdriver) is smuggling something and asks if the truckdriver will level with him on this, the guard's last day. "What were you smuggling?" asks the guard. "Trucks," replies the truckdriver.

Dr. Gitlin was using the parable to illustrate a need to concentrate on the big picture, with regard to media, and we would advocate that same focus in approaching the chapters of this book. The details and specifics of each lesson, unit, and content area are (we hope) of value and worthy of your attention. At the same time, we hope that you will keep in mind some overarching themes and principles that form a basis for the entire book:

- The most significant learning occurs when the learning matters to those involved.

- Students will be more likely to become involved and to put forth their best effort when they care about what they are doing and are clear about why they are doing it.

- Students who share with each other, in deciding what to investigate, in carrying out research, in preparing to present what they have found, and in actually presenting their research are both helping each other to learn and are learning about each other. This leads to both an increased awareness of their commonalities, hence to an increased tolerance and acceptance of each other and to an appreciation of their unique experiences and talents.

- When students are preparing to present on a topic, they must learn more than they will actually present. This causes them to have to make critical decisions about the relative importance of what they have found, and it encourages them to consider their audience when deciding what to share and how to share it.

- There is a true joy in learning about the world. When we affirm this as teachers by allowing our students to experience that joy, we foster habits of lifelong learning.

We believe that these elements are present in (and more important than) any one lesson or lesson sequence, and we hope that you maintain your awareness of them as you proceed through this book. So more than being a set of *what-to-teach* ideas, these activities are focused on *how to think* about teaching and learning. This is the truck we're driving.

Resources

Gitlin, Todd. 2002. *Media Unlimited.* New York: Metropolitan Books.
National Council for the Social Studies. 1994. Silver Springs, Maryland: NCSS

1

The Timeline of Our Lives

I suppose one of the big problems today, perhaps in all societies in the world, certainly in our society in the United States, is this break in continuity. So many of the young feel that they don't know what happened before they were born.

—Studs Terkel

*I*n Zeno's classic paradox, Achilles can never catch up to a tortoise who has even a modest headstart, no matter how swiftly he runs, for it takes Achilles a certain amount of time to catch up to the place where the tortoise began. By that time, the tortoise has moved on, maintaining a lead, however slim. History book publishers confront a somewhat related paradox. No matter how up-to-the-minute textbooks are, they can never catch up to current events. Zeno's paradox can be solved mathematically. The publishers' dilemma knows no such solution. For even as the latest textbook is being printed, bound, and shipped to distributors, new history is being made.

It is the newest history that first captures our attention. I (Jan) first wrote parts of this chapter on December 26, 2001. That day, there was talk on the news of a new Osama bin Laden tape, and of the possibility that bin Laden had died, either from illness or from U.S. bombs, sometime within the past two weeks. There was talk of amnesty for corporations that disclose illegal tax shelters to the IRS. There was discussion of widespread unemployment, of recession. There was concern that India and Pakistan might go to war and that one or both of them might use nuclear weapons. There were articles about stem cells, cloning, longevity, Alzheimer's, Epstein-Barr virus and its connection to multiple sclerosis.

Returning to this discussion nearly a year later, October 15, 2002, I typed as I listened to news of a sniper in the Washington, DC, area who just that day shot an eleventh victim. Other current news items being discussed included the prospect of an imminent war with Iraq, where they were in the midst of presidential elections and Saddam Hussein, the only candidate on the ballot, was expected to garner more than 99 percent of the votes. A tourist bar in Bali, Indonesia, had been bombed, and it was the first year anniversary of the arrival of an anthrax-laden letter sent to Senator Tom Daschle's office, a crime that remains unsolved. The World Series was shaping up as a contest between the Giants and Angels—*our* guys (the Mariners) having been eliminated before the playoffs.

A few days later, we were stricken with the news of Senator Paul Wellstone, his wife, daughter, three campaign workers, and two pilots dead in a plane crash. Half a world away, more than 700 hostages were being held in a Moscow theater by Chechen captors who threatened to blow them all up if Russia would not withdraw from Chechnya. And the World Series was set to go to a seventh game. We didn't know it yet, but by the next day, more than a hundred of the hostages and fifty of their captors would be dead and the Anaheim Angels would be the new baseball champs, at least until the next World Series.

So it goes. Each day there is news that grabs our attention. And by the time we read it, something else is on the horizon; something new is in the making. Cloned humans. Wars. New records set in sports or at the box office. New discoveries in space. By the time you read this sentence, hundreds of other headlines, large and small, will have come and gone. Some will have been predictable, some quite unforeseen. Each of them will have been important to some of us, and some of them will have been important to many of us.

Yet if we were to open most history books in most classrooms, we would find that the first chapters students study are, for the most part, about events and issues that are the furthest away in time from today's events and interests. In many classrooms, students will be asked to turn to pages in their textbooks about exploration and colonization, or ancient river valley civilizations. How many of them will even realize that the Tigris–Euphrates River Valley is none other than Iraq, where their fathers, mothers, aunts, uncles, older siblings, friends, neighbors, or even teachers may have seen combat duty? How many of them will connect a question about why Mohenjo-Daro in ancient India disappeared with questions about the effects shifting weather patterns, tectonic plate movement, floods, droughts, overpopulation, and war may have on major centers of civilization today? But the prescribed curriculum, the official scope and sequence, may not call for a focus on Twentieth- (much less Twenty-first) Century History or Contemporary World Problems until the final year of high school!

How then, can we help students make significant connections? Why worry about making significant connections anyway? For one thing, it's really the only way to remember things. If we study isolated facts and don't make connections, those facts go in one neuron and out the other, never causing enough of a stir to be sent into long-term memory. So students may study hard, cram for the quizzes, and even raise their scores on standardized tests, but ask them a year or two later what they studied, and they'll remember very little.

And really, who in their right—or left—mind would argue that students should make insignificant connections when significant ones are possible? Don't we owe it to students to answer that age-old student question—"Why do we have to study this?"—with something other than the equally age-old quip that quotes George Santayana and threatens a failing grade: "Those who cannot remember the past are condemned to repeat it"?

The Importance of Connected, Meaningful Narrative

Accumulating research in cognitive science confirms that children develop their sense of time through constructing personally meaningful narratives. When timeline skills are taught in isolation from what matters to the students, the students are less likely to remember the concept because it isn't connected to meaningful narrative. So, let us assume that it is valuable for students to make significant connections.

Connections to what? In *Best Practice: New Standards for Teaching and Learning in America's Schools* Zemelman, Daniels, and Hyde (1998) summarize several kinds of important connections: connections to students' own interests, connections to their classrooms and communities, connections to other subject and discipline areas, connections to their own prior knowledge, connections to their own backgrounds and to cultures other than their own, connections to their eventual role as engaged and informed citizens of a democracy.

This suggests that we might learn something important about teaching history by putting Zeno and his paradox aside as our model and considering instead the example provided by the White Queen in Alice's *Through the Looking Glass*. The Queen shouts "Ouch!" then bleeds, then pricks her finger. Let us begin in the here and now, where students are automatically connected to their own interests, their communities, and their prior knowledge. Let us notice what makes us shout, then ask what effect that has had on us, then query the antecedents.

Whether we gather news from newspapers and other print media, television reports, radio, or simply "what's in the air," any given day will find us more aware of some issues in the news, less aware of others. Naturally, we will pay the most attention to those issues in which we are the most interested. What catches our attention on any given day may be international in scope, national, regional, or local. It may be primarily political in nature or related to finance, crime, sports, or entertainment.

We can build essential social studies skills of learning to research and interpret timelines by starting right now, today, with what is on our collective minds and asking a few questions. In that process, we can lay the foundation for meaningful learning of social studies content from decades and centuries past as well, because students will be finding personally meaningful connections in their research, and will discover additional connections as they share their research with others.

A Note About Open-Ended Research

This is the first of several units that makes use of an open-ended research process. This process will be discussed more in detail in Chapter 4, Trading Stories. At this point, it is enough to note that as students begin to look for documents relating to their theme or topic, they may discover that something entirely different catches their attention. This is one of the joys of such research. While browsing for headlines on one issue, we see another and suddenly realize the contemporaneousness of events we'd not put together in our minds before. Encourage students to wander like this through the resources they find, and to change their original topic or theme if they find something that also fits the assignment and is more compellingly interesting to them.

The fact that open-ended research does not always lead us to expected places does not mean that it is less rigorous than the traditional model. In fact, it often requires more time and evokes more critical thinking. Students who do not find what they first set out to find often report that they invested far more time in the assignment than their counterparts. Moreover, they are often the students who are most enthused by the results.

Building Connections With Timelines

This is initially an individual research assignment. Students identify a topic or theme of interest to them in the news today, then find a historical document relating to the same topic or theme that is at least a decade or more old. They copy the document, annotate it, and bring it to class. A timeline, which has all the items researched by the students indicated on it, is constructed along with other contextualizing items. These include major historical events and eras as well as personal details such as birthdates and important family events. The initial activity can take as little as two class periods, but it can also provide a launchpad for a much longer unit, a semester, or a year-long thread.

The Steps

If the research is done as homework, allow two to four class periods for the basic activity. If teaching research skills is a necessary part of the process, adjust in-class time expectations accordingly.

1. Ask students, either in class or as homework, to read a current newspaper, watch television news, or discuss current events with friends or family.

2. In class, generate a list of all the current events that are on the minds of the students.

3. Discuss each item in terms of some of the themes or topics one might research to find historical antecedents to it. One item might generate a number of different avenues of research questioning. For example, a number of students just after the 2000 presidential election were following the controversy over the counting of votes in Florida. This could lead to the following research themes or topics, among many others: When was the last disputed presidential election? When did African Americans begin voting in large numbers in the South? Have there been efforts to disband the Electoral College system? When did voting machines become standard? What does the Constitution say about states' rights versus federal rights in federal elections?

4. Brainstorm a list of all the ways students might find historical documents relating to their query. Typically, the list will include newspaper archives at local libraries; old magazines, whether in libraries or attics and basements; Internet sites, especially those that collect and/or display facsimiles of historical documents; family scrapbooks and other memorabilia; museums; photograph collections in museums or on the Internet; and elderly friends and family members who may have been eyewitnesses to the historical events we are curious about.

5. Explain that students are to find one historical document that relates to their current interest and is at least a decade old. (For adult

students, you may choose to make this twenty-five rather than ten years.) This may be an opportune time to arrange a visit to the school library or the local public library to learn how to use the *Readers' Guide to Periodical Literature* or to the computer lab to investigate Internet resources and learn how to use them.

6. Ask the students to make a photocopy, or printout, of at least the first page of the document they find.

7. Ask students to annotate the photocopy with a couple of sentences saying what links they found, or didn't find, between the document and their original research topic. Were they surprised at what they found? Was an assumption they made reinforced or contradicted? Has there been a great deal of change related to this issue, or relatively little change?

   For example, one student researching school violence in the year of the Columbine School shootings found a headline in the *New York Times* from the 1920s that sounded very contemporary. It lamented the rise of violence in the schools, and wondered how schools could be made safer when students came with guns or knives. Very little seemed to have changed, at least from the evidence of this one article.

   On the other hand, another student, researching the move to ban cigarette smoking in public places, found a magazine ad from the forties showing a young mother, in her high heels, dress, and apron, smoking a cigarette while feeding her toddler in his high chair. Obviously, public attitudes about both smoking and dress styles for mothers have changed greatly in the intervening decades.

8. Have students meet in groups of three to five to discuss how they went about finding their documents and what they discovered.

9. Give each student a strip of tagboard, or construction paper, with instructions to put the date of their document across the top, and a

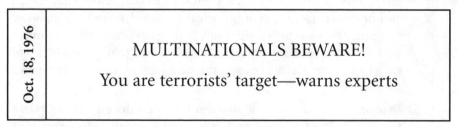

Oct. 18, 1976

MULTINATIONALS BEWARE!

You are terrorists' target—warns experts

Figure 1–1 *Each document is dated and summarized in a headline on a piece of tagboard.*

headline summarizing the document along the length of the strip, as illustrated in Figure 1–1. While they are doing this, poll the class to see who has the earliest date.

10. Create a timeline on the chalkboard, or on a length of butcher paper (the latter is preferred because it can be left on permanent display and added to later on), which includes the earliest date and is marked off by decades up through the present date (see Figure 1–2). Beginning with the earliest item, ask students to come up and attach their headlines to the timeline at the appropriate spot, while announcing their research topic and the headline for what they found. When all the items have been posted, discuss what has emerged from the collected research of the students. Are there patterns? Surprises? New questions that have come up as a result of the research?

11. Brainstorm major historical events and eras that are not yet on the timeline. Add them. You might want to use a different color of tagboard for these items, to distinguish them from the original student-researched ones. Give each student another piece of tagboard (again, perhaps a new color) on which to write their name and birthdate. Add to the timeline.

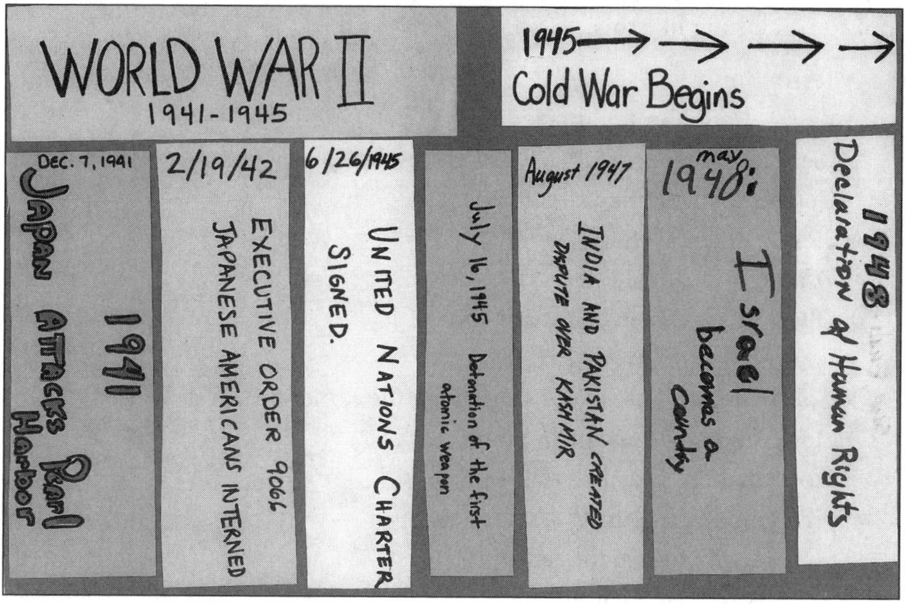

Figure 1–2 *The tagboard headlines in chronological sequence become a timeline.*

12. Discuss which historical events took place in the same years the students were born. This can be done fairly quickly, sharing what the students already know (and serving as a diagnostic assessment), or it can be done as another round of research.

Where Do Students Look for Information?

Older students can go to libraries or search Internet sites on their own. Younger students may need much more assistance and in-class support. In addition to the microfiche collections and stacks at local libraries, some publications are collections of historical documents. One such book is a collection of front pages from the first one hundred fifty years of the *New York Times*.

Local newspapers may have similar commemorative books or pamphlets. There are several collections of founding documents, one or more of which could and should be part of any school's social studies library. Thrift stores often have old magazines for very little cost; many a basement or attic is filled with old *National Geographic, Life,* or *Time* magazines. *Time* publishes commemorative issues, which include articles from decades gone by. If you are concerned that the students won't be able to find resources on their own, take some time to collect a few good books and website addresses beforehand. The resources listed at the end of this chapter will get you started.

September 2001

On a day in September 2001, the list of issues of concern in one classroom looked something like this:

- Terrorism
- World Trade Center attack
- (Seattle) Mariners record season
- Genetically modified organisms
- Stem-cell research
- Osama bin Laden
- Olympic Pipe Line Company indicted
- Food shortages in Africa
- Coho salmon—are endangered wild the same species as farmed?
- Husky football fans die in plane crash
- Stock market closed until Monday
- NFL games postponed
- Second man gets artificial heart
- Threats against local mosques

Some of the many research questions brainstormed were:

- How long have certain terrorist groups been operating?
- When and why was the World Trade Center built?
- When was the Endangered Species Act passed?
- When were stem cells first discovered?
- How does the treatment of Arab Americans parallel what happened in the past to Japanese Americans?
- When did Muslims become a significant percentage of the United States population?
- Who did the first heart transplant? Where?
- Which other baseball teams have played in Seattle?
- When was the first genetically modified organism created?
- What are other examples of disasters caused by technology, such as the Olympic Pipeline explosion?

Finding Connections, Patterns, and Changes Over Time

In our September 2001 activity, one student found information about Osama bin Laden, while another researched Timothy McVeigh and the Oklahoma City bombing. In both cases, the documents mentioned that the individuals in question were trained by the U.S. military. A third found that warnings of terrorist actions against corporations have been issued for decades.

When John Glenn made his second trip to the moon, quite a few students that year researched some aspect of the space program. We found information about women as astronauts, the impact of space travel on health, the origins of the space program in Cold War competition, and the Wright Brothers' first flight. There were women astronauts in the fifties, one student reported, but the male astronauts refused to participate in the program in those days if the women were going to be allowed to do so as well; the women were dropped. In 1903, the Wright Brothers managed to keep the first airplane in the air for up to 59 seconds, covering distances of up to 850 feet, while in 2001, NASA was working on a plane that will fly close to 5,000 mph.

A Hollywood film often inspires research. The year *Titanic* was breaking box-office records, a number of students researched the event that inspired the film. One found an article in the *New York Times* listing the casualties, another found information about efforts to recover the sunken ship, and a third located a document discussing the reasons for the accident. This connected in-class discussion to an item that had been in our local newspaper not long before about a smaller boating collision found to have been caused by human error and exhaustion.

Starting With the Students' Families

Connie Coffman, a social studies teacher at Roosevelt High School in Seattle, had her students research their ancestors. In this variation, rather than beginning with a news item of interest, the students were starting even more at the center of their own universe—with themselves! They could pick any ancestor, any number of generations back, whom they wanted to research. Alternatively, they could research their family tree in general. Students who were not comfortable with either of these assignments could propose an alternative project, such as researching their families' cultures; or, if too little was known or discoverable about their ancestors, they could research the historical circumstances that might have faced and/or surrounded an ancestor. They could also choose to research a cultural artifact in lieu of doing family history research. One student, for example, researched pirogi, a Polish meat-filled dumpling, while another investigated chocolate and was surprised to find that Swiss chocolate actually originated with the Aztecs.

To build the timeline, students were asked whose research has taken them the furthest back in history. That date became the timeline's beginning point. One student had been able to document ancestors as far back as the 1100s; most were able to locate documents from the early part of the twentieth century. Because there were far fewer items in earlier centuries, the timeline was divided into one section that stretched from 1100 to 1899, and a second one that began in 1900 and continued through to the present day.

Connie's instructions to them were as follows:

1. Find out about as many of your ancestors as possible.

2. Choose one person related to you to learn about.

3. Through primary sources (their diaries or letters, people who knew them, photographs, their possessions, etc.) and secondary sources (books, articles about them, etc.) find out the following:

   • As much of their life story as possible (personal characteristics, events in their life, their beliefs, etc.)

   • The geography of where they lived (include the land, climate, plants, animals, crops, etc.)

   • Current events of that area of the world

   • The history/time period in which they lived (social movements, leaders, events, etc.)

4. Prepare a class presentation in which you will attempt to make this person come alive. Be creative as you present him or her to us. You can bring artifacts—clothes, pictures, food, music, and so on. You may do this on your own or work with up to two other students to gather the country information. You will each present your person individually.

Students prepared a ten- to fifteen-minute presentation that either explicated their family tree, in general, or told the in-depth story of a particular ancestor. As the students shared their stories, their classmates asked questions. Concluding the presentation, the students answered their choice of three questions from a list of eight about how they do or don't feel connected to and/or influenced by their ancestors.

As they presented, there were also questions about how they found their information, and they shared research sources with each other. One student who had little to go on other than his parents' names and a grandparent's name on each side, discovered information at *www.ancestry.com*. (*Note:* This site offers a free trial membership, but it must be canceled within fourteen days to avoid the annual fee.) This led to a discussion of the websites maintained by the Mormon Church. One Mormon boy shared the importance of family history and genealogy in his community. He knows someone, he told the class, for whom the genealogy records are so important that she carries them with her at all times so that they are not vulnerable to theft or fire.

Fascinating glimpses into the extraordinary experiences of ordinary people came out through these presentations. As one student reflected, "I was surprised at how many amazing people were part of my classmates' families, and I found even the most *ordinary* families can have interesting stories to tell." There were stories of ancestors who made and lost fortunes, who struggled through history's hard times, who fled wars, who were related to some of the more familiar names in the textbooks. One boy has an ancestor from the Ross family to which Betsy Ross belonged.* One told of a slaveholding ancestor who was murdered by his slaves because he treated them so unfairly. Another told of an ancestor who, riding in one of the first automobiles, came to an abrupt stop at a railroad crossing where his false teeth flew out of his mouth and hit the side of the passing train.

Some of the students' investigations hit dead-ends when they uncovered evidence of hidden ancestors. A boy of predominantly Scandinavian ethnicity talked about two ancestors who may have been partially Native American,

---

*Ross is widely credited with designing and sewing the first American flag, though recent research suggests that she may have sewn for the troops, but did not design or sew the flag.

but noted that this was at a time in our history when people who identified themselves as white considered it a scandal, instead of a source of pride, to be part Native American. It's too bad, he commented, because the stories of those ancestors are now lost to the family.

When the presentations were concluded, the timeline was constructed. A length of butcher paper was hung in the hallway with centuries marked off. Students selected items from their reports, including photographs, and placed them on the timeline. They wrote captions, which connected the images and headlines to their own lives, directly on the paper. (See Figure 1–3.)

At the top of the butcher paper, slips of paper were added to headline contextualizing historical events and eras. The students placed their own lives on the timelines also, noting their dates of birth and adding baby pictures and other photos of themselves. Through class discussion, other significant historical eras and events were identified and added to the timeline, and the students were asked to look for patterns, connections, and questions that might be the basis for further research (see Figure 1–4). The timeline stayed on display in the hallway outside Connie's classroom, became a point of interest for others passing by, and generated discussion among both students and faculty about the possibility of an all-school timeline.

Figure 1–3 *Students wrote captions connecting items on the timeline to their own lives.*

Extensions

In addition to the family history research project, the following are a number of ways to extend or vary the basic timeline exercise.

- *Keep the timeline on display throughout the school year.* With each unit of study, add the significant dates and/or events from it to the timeline.

- *Do another round of research.* As students generate new questions from their first round of research, have them locate new documents. Add the new dates and headlines to the timeline.

- *Interview family members.* Find out which historical events they've lived through. Add their birthdates or life spans and headline/summary statements about the events to the timeline.

- *Build timeline elements into other assignments.* If students are reading biographies, have them create timelines for the person about whom they are reading. Include on it not only the important events in the life of the person, but the important historical events that were happening in the world at the same time to help students continue to build an appreciation for historical context.

- *Life timelines.* Have each student create a timeline of his or her own life, showing the birthdate as the beginning and including at least five

Figure 1–4 *In this timeline, students wrote captions directly on butcher paper rather than on tag board strips.*

significant events or changes in the student's life (e.g., moves, starting school, birth of siblings, meeting a good friend, death of a grandparent, a family vacation). *A note of caution:* Be sensitive to the fact that some students may have painful times in their lives that they will not want to share or think about. Support students so that they choose whatever details they want; don't insist that they include any particular kind of item. For a creative alternative way to construct a personal timeline, see Tarry Lindquist's description of the Yakama Time Ball in *Ways That Work* (1997).

• *Class timelines.* Create and maintain a timeline of significant events in the life of the classroom during the school year.

• *Future timelines.* Either as a stand-alone activity, or an extension of an existing timeline, add a section that shows the future. What predictions might the students make about headlines we'll see five, ten, fifty, or a hundred years from now? What goals do they hope to achieve, and by when?

• *Extend the research options in the family history project.* At the end of the project in Connie Coffman's class, students were asked to reflect on their learning experience and also to make suggestions for improving the project. Elise B. proposed adding another option for students to choose—researching a specific historical incident or event that had a significant impact on an ancestor.

But What About the Prescribed Scope and Sequence?

Creating a timeline that begins in the here and now does not mean you have to abandon an adopted textbook's chronology, or a prescribed scope and sequence. It can also be shaped to the particular course you are teaching. Whatever the subject, the topics students are interested in and bring to the timeline can give context to the basic curriculum, especially if the timeline is left on display and extended to include events that are studied throughout the course.

Mike Sullivan, a teacher in Chico, California, begins his United States History course by asking the students when they were born, when their parents were born, when their grandparents were born, and so on. As they plot the years back through the decades, they see that they may well have had an ancestor or ancestors who were personally affected by the Civil War, that tracing them back further could lead to a connection to the Revolutionary War. Even if they didn't yet live in what was to become the United States, they were alive somewhere in the world, and wherever that was, it is likely someone was affected in one way or another by what was going on here on this continent.

Even this briefest of timeline discussions serves to help the students feel a connection to the material they will be studying in their textbook. In an e-mail to us Sullivan writes:

> At some point every year, a friend spams me with a much circulated e-mail, bemoaning what the entering group of college freshman don't know about recent history. From where I sit, applying that same criterion to each year's group of thirteen-year-olds is especially sobering, therefore I am very mindful of my audience. I was going through some old pictures recently, and was troubled about how much I don't know about the people I came from. I am looking at the images of my relatives, and I don't know who they are. If learning to understand my past is a challenge, how much more will it be for a teenager coping with the onslaught of media-driven popular culture. If I want my students to genuinely love history, then I have to help them connect to it at a personal level; it has to become their history.
>
> By constructing a timeline-matrix that identifies the scope of that history, along with their parents', and grandparents' lives, we have a point of reference from which we can begin to understand what came before us. There is a natural disconnection from our past that can be overcome, if we start from what we know. All of history's great events happened to someone from whom we are descended.
>
> History is personal; you just have to make the connection.

The Bridge to the Twenty-First Century and Beyond

When I (Jan) was in high school, my teachers struggled to get up to World War II. Usually, the year ended right about the time we were beginning that chapter in the text. The Korean War was not yet part of the published narrative, even though it was almost a decade in the past. History seemed very, well, historical—like something that ended back then. Although my father fought in World War II, I had little sense that anything I was studying in my history class had much to do with his life or mine.

It's a persistent problem. No matter how current the materials, there is always that gap, whether large or small, between what the texts and materials tell us and what is happening today. And there is an even greater gap between what is happening today and what might happen tomorrow. There's a curse, allegedly Chinese, that says, "May you live in interesting times." And we do. Whether it is a curse or a blessing remains to be seen. We live at a time in history when the rate of change is dizzying and the issues that face us are enormous.

Futurists tell us that the rate of change we can reasonably expect to see in the next twenty-five to fifty years will be as much as we've seen in the entire twentieth century. We might take another cue from the White Queen in *Through the Looking Glass,* and practice believing six impossible things before breakfast, because by suppertime they might have come true. The students who are in our classrooms today, for whom the Vietnam War is ancient history —that is, it happened before they were born, and perhaps even before their parents were born—are the ones whose lifetimes will be lived almost entirely in that accelerating era of change.

All the more reason, then, to help students make sense out of it all by seeing the connected narrative of history. Connecting what matters to *us* today, and to who *we* are today, with what brought us here from the past, is a crucial part of preparing adequately for the future.

Resources

Books and Printed Materials

Grun, Bernard, and Daniel J. Boorstin. 1991. *The Timetables of History: A Horizontal Linkage of People and Events, Third Edition.* New York: Touchstone Books.

Lindquist, Tarry. 1997. *Ways That Work.* Portsmouth, NH: Heinemann.

Urdang, Laurence, and Arthur Meier Schlesinger Jr. 2001. *The Timetables of American History, Millennium Edition.* New York: Touchstone Books.

New York Times (ed.). 2001. *The New York Times Page One 1851–2001: Special Commemorative Edition Celebrating 150 Years of The New York Times.* New York: Galahad Books.

Zemelman, Steven, Harvey Daniels, and Arthur Hyde. 1998. *Best Practice: New Standards for Teaching and Learning in America's Schools, Second Edition.* Portsmouth, NH: Heinemann.

Zinn, Howard, and George Kirschner. 1995. *A People's History of the United States: The Wall Charts.* New York: New Press.

Websites

www.ancestorhunt.com/ancestry.html— This site has a fourteen-day free trial period that must be canceled to avoid incurring charges.

www.archives.gov/research_room/genealogy/about_genealogy_research.html— National Archives and Records Administration website, includes tips on how to begin to do genealogical research and a bibliography of books on genealogy.

www2.canisius.edu/~emeryg/time.html— AlternaTime, a collection of links to a wide variety of timelines on the World Wide Web.

www.familysearch.org/— Mormon (Latter Day Saints) website with free searchable database.

http://genealogy.about.com/mbody.htm— Includes links to information about where to locate vital records, such as birth certificates, marriage licenses, death certificates.

http://genealogy.about.com/library/weekly/aa110800a.htm?PM=ss14_genealogy— A list of links to twenty-five free sites for researching genealogy.

www.ourtimelines.com/— Personalized timelines; this site allows you to enter your personal data; it then generates a personal timeline for you that includes historical events as well as your entries.

http://timelines.ws/—Timelines of History, links by date and subject matter.

2

I, Witness to History

There is no such thing as a neutral or purely objective historian.
Without an opinion a historian would be simply a ticking clock,
and unreadable besides.

—Barbara W. Tuchman

Chicago. 1964. A protester against the war in Vietnam was found guilty today
of failure to carry his draft card at all times and failure to comply with induc-
tion procedures. Denying a defense motion that Robert Switzer remain free
pending sentencing, presiding Judge Julius Hoffman declared "I will not be a
party to allowing this dangerous criminal to roam the streets of Chicago spread-
ing his doctrine of the violent overthrow of the United States government."

Switzer, an avowed total pacifist whose views are deeply influenced by Mahatma
Gandhi and Martin Luther King, went limp. United States deputy marshal
Eugene Bissell dragged him by his feet out of the courtroom. As his head
bounced on the marble floor, Switzer's sister became distraught and cried,
"Stop! You're hurting him!" An elderly man who'd watched the two-week trial
retorted, "Serves him right." A second woman turned to the man and asked,
incredulously, "How can you call him dangerous?"

I (Jan) was that second woman, and this is my version of the events. It differs
in significant detail from a previously published version, which I will discuss
in a moment.

25

I grew up in central Indiana during the fifties. I was a good social studies student, especially in my middle and high school years. My seventh-grade teacher indulged my penchant for discourse and allowed me to hone my critical thinking skills by debating him on current events issues. My eighth-grade teacher exposed us to powerful Anti-Defamation League teaching materials about the Holocaust, about racism in the United States, and how prejudice colors our perception of events. My tenth-grade teacher was a conservative Republican who'd been grilled by the House Committee on Un-American Activities because he dared use supplementary materials, which included the non-Western world materials his accusers had not read, for his world history course. He inspired me with his insistence on our right to the free flow of ideas and information.

During my first year of college, I became active, as did so many, in questioning our country's involvement in Vietnam. Throughout it all, I maintained my firm belief in the concept that each of us was guaranteed our day in court, and that news articles, as contrasted to editorials, were relatively neutral accounts of events.

The day I saw my friend convicted in a courtroom where the judge's bias would later make history (it was Judge Hoffman who would preside over the trial of the Chicago Seven, and order one codefendant, Bobby Seale, bound and gagged in the courtroom), I was deeply shaken. When I read the account of the trial in the *Chicago Tribune* the next day, I was floored. The *Tribune*'s account stated: "Friends of Switzer who had sat thru the trial followed Bissell, shouting imprecations at the United States marshal." I didn't even know what imprecations were, but I looked them up—*imprecation:* a spoken curse, a malediction, said the dictionary. Through the power of the press, my determinedly nonviolent friend's distressed sister and I were made to sound like a disruptive mob, hurling evil threats at uniformed representatives of the U.S. government. That account, of course, is the one that remains in history. My account, reconstructed here, has heretofore been unavailable to the public.

The History of the Class

The activities described in this chapter are meant to engage students in two ways. First, we hope they will come to realize that each of us is both an eyewitness to history and a participant in making history, and that our accounts are important pieces of the historical record. Second, we hope they will become critical consumers of the histories they read and hear, asking questions that take them deeper into developing the habits of historians.

We begin with a fairly simple little exercise called The History of the Class. It's best to set this up after a given group of students has had time to share some common experiences, say halfway or more through a particular class. It's also going to work best if the students are asked to write anonymously. This generally gives them more room to play with the exercise, which in turn evokes a wider range of samples.

Each student writes a history of the class from his or her point of view. The teacher moderates a discussion about historical source documents, and who is and isn't typically included in history accounts, using the examples written by the students.

The Steps

1. Ask the students to write a brief history of the class thus far. Encourage students to think about the most important aspects of the class and to select what they write about accordingly, because they will have only a short time to complete their accounts. With adults, ten or fifteen minutes is generally sufficient. High school and middle school students will probably require twenty or so. If they ask about formatting requirements, or titling requirements, answer open-endedly: "However you define it." "However you want to set it up." "Whatever you think it is important to include." "This is your history, so I can't tell you what's important in it." Again, encourage them to write anonymously, so that they feel free to write the truth as they see it. Very occasionally, a student will choose to write something inappropriate about another student or a teacher. If you know this is likely to happen and you've discussed this issue before with the student or the class, you might want to give the student a brief reminder. Otherwise, you can address it if it comes up as you read the accounts by explaining that you won't read anything that would embarrass or humiliate any member of the class.

2. When the majority of students have completed their accounts, give a one- or two-minute warning, and then ask them to finish up whatever sentence they're on, turn their papers face down, and pass them in.

3. Put the papers aside for the moment, and ask students to consider that it is perhaps twenty-five or thirty years in the future. (You can adjust this depending on the age of the students, but keep it within a range so that it is possible people with firsthand knowledge of the class would still be alive.) What kinds of events might happen in those years?

   As students voice ideas, list them on the board or an overhead. Generally, ideas can be sorted into a number of categories: natural disasters such as earthquakes, volcano eruptions, floods, fires, and draughts; political events such as elections, wars, coups, and terrorist attacks; public health disasters such as epidemics of various diseases; events caused by people and/or their technologies such as fires or airplane crashes, but also new inventions and technologies such as cloning, computer-enhanced intelligence, and cures for diseases. This is by no means an exhaustive list, and all suggestions should be added to the list. If no one is voicing an idea in a particular category, you can get ideas flowing by asking a guiding question—"What about natural disasters?" or "What about changes due to advances in science?"

4. Now gather all the histories that have been written and shuffle them. Refer to the reasons listed on the board as you announce that this one or that one has met, at least temporarily, the fate of being lost. As you give a reason, put those histories aside; or, if you've a flair for the dramatic, toss them over your shoulder or let them drop to the floor. "These were lost in the flood of ought four. These went up in flames in 2010. These were suppressed because the government didn't like what they said. This bunch was chewed up by mice and turned into nesting material. These got rained on. A couple of them got zapped when aliens invaded. This one was recycled, this one was hidden in Grandma's attic . . ." and so forth. Use ideas that the students have brainstormed, or any others that strike you as amusing or useful, until you are holding a single document.

5. Announce with a great flourish that this document, therefore, is "The Official History of the Class—the only known account of a historical event." And it is . . . Read the document aloud. (If, by any chance, the document is inappropriate for reading aloud, you can simply say that it, too, was suppressed. Then pull another document from the pile, saying that this one has just been discovered.)

6. Lead students in a discussion to sort out apparent facts and opinions, and list questions that the document raises.

7. Repeat the process of *discovering* documents until there are enough to have a variety of approaches and some overlapping details. Discuss where one might go to do further research on the historical event referred to in the documents.

8. Lead a discussion about how it feels if your account is chosen as one of the *official* histories of the class, and how it feels if your account is

never heard or read by others. Relate this to the points of view typically represented in history books and the points of view typically ignored or given only token attention.

A *general note:* Based on our experience, at least half of the time you will find yourself reading a document that has little by way of cut-and-dried dates and facts but is rich in a personal point of view. Other times, you'll have a document that is very *fact*-oriented, with a timeline, perhaps, and a list of topics and dates that the class covered. Either way works. If students ask whether they can use their notes, discourage this. Otherwise, you are likely to get mostly lists of topics and/or recapitulations of assignments rather than the rich and engaging array of personal accounts that reflect the great individuality of the people writing the histories.

Discovering and Debriefing the Documents

Here's how a debriefing sequence might work if the first document is highly subjective and/or incomplete. These documents were adapted from an integrated curriculum methods course for preservice teachers; the names have been changed, as Sergeant Friday of Dragnet fame used to say, to protect the innocent.

Document 1

> 1/28—Physical space
>
> Demographics
>
> Perspective
>
> Relation to our things
>
> Mind mapping (concept maps)
>
> School mapping
>
> How to make the schoolyard a better environment for everyone
>
> 1/30—Cultural Scavenger Hunt: It started on a glorious forlorn wet Seattle night at Northwood Elem. That was where we came to know the magnificent Matthew Martinson. I grinned to myself as I overheard the exclamations of two companions who swooned with delight.

Of course, when one reads a document like this aloud, having announced it as The Official History of the Class, there is generally laughter. We recognize immediately that a phrase, such as "swooned with delight," is highly subjective and personal. So the first thing I might do in discussing it is to ask students to consider each bit of information in it and decide whether it is probably fact or probably opinion. Distinguishing fact and opinion is a key social studies skill. (I fret when I hear or read someone using the phrase "I agree with the fact . . ." as if a fact is something one can reasonably either agree with or disagree with.) So we come up with a tentative agreement that 1/28, the date, is probably a fact. (Of course a person can always be mistaken about the date, or lie about it, but we'll assume for the moment that this one is, indeed, a fact.) The list we have to reserve judgment on. There's not quite enough there to allow us to determine with full confidence. But we think it's probably more fact than opinion. Another date, 1/30, another presumed fact. The phrase "a glorious forlorn wet Seattle night" seems to contain two opinions (glorious and forlorn) and two facts (wet Seattle). We assume, too, that it was a "night" can be taken as fact. Moving on through the document, "Matthew Martinson" is probably a fact. That he is "magnificent" would have to be, for the moment, classified as opinion. That the writer "grinned" as he or she listened to comments is probably a fact. Whether the companions actually "swooned with delight" is a little harder to figure out, without more data.

I list each of these various details under one of three columns: Known Facts, Opinions, Not Clear. Then we consider what questions the document raises for us. We come up with a list: What began on that "glorious forlorn wet night"? Who is the illustrious Matthew Martinson? Who is the writer who "grinned"? What sort of group was meeting? Why were they meeting at Northwood Elem? Can we assume this refers to Northwood Elementary School? What does the list signify? Why is it dated two days earlier than the paragraph that presumably tells when it all started? This apparently happened in January, but of what year? Summarizing, we know with fair accuracy the *where* of this event, but the *who, why,* and *how* are still pretty much unknowns.

"But wait!" I announce, while pulling another document from the pile. "There's been a new discovery! Another document has been found, close enough to the site of the first that there is reason to suspect that it may refer to the same event. Let's see what it says." I read the next document aloud.

Document 2

Moving things–Immovable things–Holy things

97 Curriculum B

Life faces us with transformations, full of change. For long it has been the way to do things has been fixed. But how we have come far the children of tomorrow.

Hmmmm. This document reveals, first of all, that primary source documents don't always come to us fully edited, nor even fully legible. These are the words, as best as I can make them out, but perhaps the phrase is "now we have come for the children of tomorrow."

First drafts of anyone's documents are often full of such ambiguities, because our brains operate many times more rapidly than our fingers do in recording our thoughts. And our handwriting may not win any penmanship awards. For the moment, we'll let these ambiguities stand and see whether there is any evidence that this document refers to the same event as the first one did. There really doesn't seem to be evidence to that effect.

Only one or two elements emerge as possible *facts*. That this is something to do with "97 Curriculum B," whatever that is, and that life, at least in this writer's perception, is full of changes, facing us with transformations.

The document raises a couple of new questions. What does "Moving things–Immovable things–Holy things" refer to? What do tomorrow's children have to do with this writer?

Fortunately, we needn't ponder these too long without new input, for our attention is captured by a third document, which has just come to light. As before, I pull a document at random from the heap and read it to the students.

Document 3

> "And . . . Freeze!" Most of us stopped, gasping for breath. A few stumbled on a step or two. I couldn't remember when I last ran like that. And for the first time since I was nine, I was doing it smiling. I went home truly exhilarated that I finally had a class I was going to enjoy.
>
> At our next session, we presented our activities and did soccer drills. I went home wanting to be a soccer coach, if I could manage to learn to play the game.
>
> All the PE classes were wonderful—I was into PE like never before in my life.
>
> Generally, the good feelings kept up—or maybe I should call it spirit.

Still no answers to our original questions. Are there any hints that document 3 is either about the same event referred to as document 1 or document 2? Not really! We list the perceived facts:

> It's about a class.
>
> The writer is older than 9, perhaps adult.
>
> It's a PE class. The participants did soccer drills and activities.

New questions emerge:

- Who was calling "Freeze?"
- Who is the "we" referred to?
- How many years has the author run—however infrequently—without a smile?
- In what context did the good feelings or spirit continue?

At this point, our best guess might be that the documents refer to three entirely separate events. We press on. I take another page from the pile, announcing that a fourth document has literally "turned up."

Document 4

Physical Education Professor—Matthew Martinson

Place—Northwood Elementary School

Time—Jan. 6, 1997 – Jan. 21, 1997

Attendants—24 students

Found out about activities, exercises, methods for PE

Social Studies Professor—Jan Maher

Science Professor—Bill Rhodes

Place—Central Community College

Time—Jan. 24, 1997

At last we have some very specific details: names, dates, places. And we can start making some tentative connections. Northwood appears in documents 1 and 4. Matthew Martinson appears in 1, 3, and 4; references to PE and/or physical activities are made in documents 1, 3, and 4. Hints that there are sessions relating to more than one area of curriculum are there in documents 1 and 4. The year 1997 appears in 2 and 4; reference to schools and/or children appear in documents 1, 2, and 4.

There are some date ambiguities. At this point, 1/6, 1/21, 1/24, 1/28, and 1/30 have been mentioned, plus the information in document 3 that at least the PE class met more than once, probably three or more times. Document 4 suggests that it met from January 6 through January 21.

Let's take a look at one more discovered document.

Document 5

The quarter started with PE taught by Matthew Martinson (he told us to call him "Matt").

There were five class sessions, over 2 $\frac{1}{2}$ weeks. It was a good class, enjoyable, but much more challenging physically than many of us were prepared for. Also, we didn't expect so much homework. Matt was very fair in his grading system, though, so we didn't mind.

We also had math once a week, which was an extension of last quarter's math class. The same instructor taught it. One night he sported a big button that, if you can believe what one witness reported, might have said "Poke me I'm squishy."

We've got a new and intriguing detail with the introduction of the math instructor, but the common thread of Matthew Martinson seems to suggest that this document fits with the others.

How might we proceed if we wanted to find out more? Where could we look for information? We brainstorm a list: Search public records, such as the Internet and phone books, for names, especially Matthew Martinson. See whether we can locate the people named and interview them. Search records of space usage at Northwood Elementary School for January 1997. Who rented the space? Especially the gymnasium? If there is no longer a Northwood Elementary School in the city in which the documents were found, of course we'd have a little more digging to do just to find out when and where Northwood Elementary existed. We might also be prepared to search other school districts in the area to see whether there is more than one Northwood Elementary School. We could search records of Central Community College— probably Seattle Central Community College—for courses taught in winter quarter of 1997. As it happens, this would be a dead-end because, although the class met there, it was actually a Western Washington University class.

If we found out that Western Washington University rented the gymnasium at Northwood Elementary, we could search WWU records and payroll records for the instructors' names, catalogue records for same, cross-referencing to courses taught and syllabus archives that would tell us more about the overall scope of Western Washington programs. We would be on the lookout for some of the terms we noticed in documents 1 and 2.

If we found Matthew Martinson, we might be able to determine the name of the course, find a class list, and search for the people who were registered in the class. We might be able to determine, then, whether anyone actually swooned or remembered anyone else swooning.

One of the interesting aspects of our chance drawings of histories is that we are hungry for some facts and figures by the time we get them in documents 4 and 5. Indeed, we might swoon with delight to get our hands on some very specific facts at this point. It's important to note this. This approach to teaching social studies doesn't eschew facts. It creates an appetite for relevant, significant facts that, by virtue of their recognized relevance and significance, are more easily remembered than ones not so recognized.

Suppose, for example, that I present you with these facts:

> Spring quarter, 1997, 23 Western Washington University students studied Health and PE methods with Matthew Martinson at Northwood Elementary School. They subsequently studied social studies methods with Jan Maher, science methods with Bill Rhodes, and math methods with an unnamed math professor. After the Health and PE sequence, they met at Seattle Central Community College.

Now I give you a little quiz (don't cheat!):

> Multiple choice—The school where the PE classes were taught was
> a) Northwood Elementary
> b) Seattle Central Community College
> c) Northgarten Elementary
> d) Northgate Elementary
>
> Matching—Match the subject on the left with the instructor who taught it on the right:
>
> | | |
> |---|---|
> | social studies | Bill Rhodes |
> | math | Matthew Martinson |
> | science | Jan Maher |
> | PE | unnamed professor |
>
> Short answer questions:
> • How many students were there?
> • What was the name of the college they attended?

You may have scored poorly on this quiz. You may have scored well. The main question in either case is *so what*? Without the stories of human responses to the class, there is no particular value to it. It is precisely because people grinned; swooned; felt a connection to tomorrow's children; felt a sense of energy, of spirit; felt physically challenged; felt inspired to coach soccer; were engaged in the question of what is and is not a fair grading system that the more cut-and-dried facts assume some kind of importance.

Yet, as we saw in the first three documents, the record is frustratingly incomplete if it is only the subjective accounts without the dates and names to anchor it. *We need both.* If we have only names and dates, we have the dried husk of history. If we have only subjective responses, feeling states, opinions, and attitudes, there's no moorage.

When the Facts Turn Up First

Now, let's look at how it might go if the first document is the fact-filled one (document 4). We list the known or presumed facts:

Matthew Martinson teaches Health/PE

Jan Maher teaches social studies

Bill Rhodes teaches science

The PE classes meet at Northwood Elementary 1/6 through 1/21

Science and social studies apparently met at Central Community College on 1/24

Year, 1997

There were 24 students

We list the apparent opinions—there don't seem to be any. This is a pretty cut-and-dried account. We list our unanswered questions:

Who were the students?

What were they preparing for?

Was the school or program a good one?

What did the participants think?

What qualified the instructors to be in their positions?

Did science and social studies only meet one time, or is 1/24 just the beginning of those classes?

We draw a second document from the pile. Suppose, for the sake of this discussion, that it is what we have called document 2. There is only the most fragile, tentative connection between the documents, and that is the year 1997. (We are assuming, even to make this connection, that 97 refers to 1997.) We generate our questions about document 2, and proceed, as we did previously, to list facts, opinions, ambiguities, and questions raised until we begin to see the same kinds of connections emerge. At this point, the following are several important questions to discuss:

- How did it feel if your history was selected as "The Official History of the Class"?
- How did it feel if your history was one of the others selected?
- How did it feel if your history was never selected?
- Which points of view are missing in the history thus far?

 The brainstormed list in answer to this question can include not only the other members of the class whose histories are still "undiscovered," but

also, the instructor of the class; the various people in supervisory capac-
ities over the class at the college; the custodial staff of the building in
which the class takes place; the family members of the people who are in
the class; the educational professionals in the community who have
strong ideas about how such a class should be taught; the family
members of the instructors; the members of the educational community
who teach similar topics at other institutions; the politicians, educators,
and community leaders who hammer out standards for the subject areas
covered; the politicians who set standards by law; the future students of
the preservice teachers who are in the class; and so forth.

• What if any one of the writers had a particular agenda?

• What if any one of the writers was simply mistaken?

• What if any one of the writers was outright lying?

Consideration of these questions brings us to the overarching guiding question of the exercise: How can we put together an accurate, fair, and inclusive
picture of what has happened in history? For other activities that address this
question, see Chapter 5, The Media: Servant of (Too?) Many Masters—particularly the textbook analysis activity.

Extensions

This activity can stand alone or can be the launchpad for a more extended
unit.

1. In the Timeline activity, we researched a theme or topic by finding a
single historical source document. We can revisit those documents
now and ask some of these same questions. Was the document a
factual one? Have the *facts* changed since the document was first
published? What kinds of opinions are embedded in the document?
What point of view is being expressed? What are some of the points
of view that are missing in the document? And so forth.

2. At this point, students are often clamoring to hear the rest of the
histories. Depending on your overall course plan, you can discover
them all at once, then move on to your next unit or lesson, or you can
discover one or two a day over the next several days or weeks. Once
all the documents have been discovered, you can hammer out the
most inclusive history of the class possible, or the most commonly
agreed-on history of the class, or you can look for the greatest contrast
in the versions of the class afforded by the histories.

   In a different semester from the one that generated the samples in
this chapter, I did this exercise later in the course sequence, after we'd

had a number of social studies sessions and a number of science sessions. One of the first histories I pulled from the pile to read declared that the social studies sessions were a disappointing waste of time. The writer expressed a wish that we'd covered social studies content rather than methods. The writer went on to say that the science sessions, by contrast, had been useful, wonderful, engaging. The very next document declared that—you guessed it—the science sessions had been a colossal waste of time, but the social studies sessions had been wonderful, useful, informative . . . (You can see why it's important to have these done anonymously.)

3. You can also relate this activity to the collage activity discussed in Chapter 3. You might return to this discussion after doing that activity, or simply refer to the quotes (see pages 43–45). How would the history of the class be written differently if it were written by Marx? How would he see class struggle expressed in the classroom? By Sir Thomas Carlyle? Would he recognize the contributions of only those who are male leaders? By James Baldwin? What would he identify as the *traps* that we are in, or that are in us? By Willa Cather? What is in our hearts, at the heart of our classroom experience together? Which details might each select? Which might each overlook? This can be just a discussion, or a full-blown assignment, with individuals or small groups taking very specific and strong points of view, and writing versions of the class through those lenses, whether they be rose-colored, emerald green, or dark.

4. Select an historical event that is part of the content of the course in which you do this activity. Locate several primary source documents that express divergent points of view. Discuss and/or process them as you did The History of the Class documents written by the students. Which elements in each document are facts? Which are opinions? Which voices are still not present in the discoverable texts? What questions do we still have? How would we go about finding possible answers to those questions? The following are a few ideas of events that would afford this opportunity:

U.S./NORTH AMERICAN HISTORY

Battle of the Alamo

U.S. invasion of the Philippines

Writing of/signing of the Declaration of Independence

Dropping of the atomic bomb on Hiroshima and Nagasaki

Brown vs. the Board of Education of Topeka, Kansas and subsequent school desegregation

U.S. escalated involvement in Vietnam following the Gulf of Tonkin incident

2000 presidential election Florida vote recount

First lunar landing

Columbus' "discovery" of America

Detention of noncitizens by the U.S. government subsequent to September 11

WORLD HISTORY

The Crusades

The War of the Roses

The Holocaust (Nazi campaign to exterminate Jewish people)

The voyage of Marco Polo

The colonization of Africa by European powers

The apartheid system in South Africa

The end of the apartheid system in South Africa

STATE HISTORIES

Conflicts and cooperation between indigenous peoples and European settlers

Legal status of slavery and/or escaped slaves

Tensions between industrialization and environmental concerns

Tensions over land use (e.g., farmers and ranchers; or industrial waste in residential areas)

Tensions over labor issues (e.g., in Washington State a wide range of published points of view are discoverable concerning the General Strike of 1919)

ECONOMICS

Trade issues (tariffs, NAFTA, fast track, etc.)

Development issues (macro- versus microeconomics)

Taxation issues (flat tax, graduated income tax, sales tax)

GEOGRAPHY

Land use issues

Resource use issues

Cultural conflicts

CONTEMPORARY WORLD ISSUES

The Chechen separatist movement

Chemical and biological weapons

Stem-cell research

Genetically modified organisms

5. This next activity is closely related to the parallel newspapers' project described in Chapter 5, The Media: Servant of (Too?) Many Masters. Find a photograph in the news that shows several figures in differing roles, such as the one in Figure 2–1 that was taken at Kent State University in 1971.

Display the photograph without any caption. Ask students to write three rounds of captions. For the first one, ask them simply to describe what they see happening in the photograph without judgment or interpretation. In the second, ask them to describe the event from the point of view of a specific figure in the image. In the third, ask that they take a particular political or ideological point of view and describe the image in a way that reflects that bias.

An interesting example of this came to us by way of Adrian Flynn who lives in Germany and reads several international news sources.

Figure 2–1 *Students can write captions from a variety of points of view to explore the various versions of history that are implicit in the scene.* © 1970 Howard E. Ruffner.

He reports that sometime in late 1990 or early 1991 he saw the same photograph in two different newspapers. The picture showed Albanian refugees who had fled by boat to Bari, Italy. Because there were so many of them, authorities had used the local football stadium for temporary shelter. In the photograph, both refugees and caribinieri (semi-military police) were visible. In the Italian paper, Adrian reports, the caption described the police as passing out food to the refugees; in the *International Tribune*, he recalls, the caption referred to the police as "brutalizing" the Albanians.

6. For a kinesthetic variation on this theme, have students create tableaus of images taken either from the newspapers or from illustrations in their social studies texts. Alternatively, they can create their own image of historical or contemporary situations. Interview each one from his or her point of view within the tableau. What is going on from that particular point of view? For example, if students create a tableau of demonstrators and police confronting one another, with passersby looking on, what will the scene look like from the point of view of a demonstrator? A law officer? A person watching from the sidelines? For a more detailed explication of this activity, see *Living History in the Classroom* (Selwyn 1993).

Fostering Thinking Skills

Expectations of Excellence: Curriculum Standards for Social Studies suggests that the skills for interpreting information, drawing inferences from factual material, recognizing the value dimension of interpreting, and recognizing instances in which more than one interpretation is possible should have major or intense emphasis at the secondary level. The activities in this chapter and those in Chapter 3, Lenses, are all designed to provide opportunities to build these skills, which can be developed further by using the activities described in Chapter 5, The Media: Servant of (Too?) Many Masters.

Resources

National Council for the Social Studies. *Expectations of Excellence: Curriculum Standards for Social Studies.* 1994. Silver Springs, Maryland: NCSS.
Selwyn, Douglas. 1993. *Living History in the Classroom.* Tucson, AZ: Zephyr Press.

3

Lenses

Most people see what they want to, or at least what they expect to.

—Martha Grimes

A popular song of a bygone decade suggests that to see the world as a rosy place, we need simply look at it through rose-colored glasses. An old saw reminds us that to a hammer, everything looks like a nail. (Perhaps to a nervous nail, everything looks like a hammer!) A Mexican proverb tells us that in this world there is neither truth nor lie, that everything is like the color of the crystal through which you gaze. The Bard of Avon agrees, asserting that there is nothing either good or bad, but thinking makes it so. The observation runs through the ages and through cultures: *How* we see significantly affects *what* we see. This chapter takes up the way in which philosophical, ideological, and cultural lenses shape our picture of reality, and how we can stretch that picture of reality so that it is a more inclusive one.

The National Council for the Social Studies (NCSS 1994) notes the importance of students learning to "accept and fulfill social responsibilities associated with citizenship in a free society," and "participate in persuading, compromising, debating, and negotiating in the resolution of conflicts and differences." It is also generally understood that in order to persuade, compromise, debate, and negotiate, we need to be able to see issues not only from our own point of view, but from that of others.

An informed democracy depends on this skill of citizenry; it is a basic premise of our legislative and judicial institutions. It's not easy to do because there is no such thing as a commonly perceived, totally objective reality. I am not suggesting that there is no objective reality, rather that we humans are incapable of perceiving it without distorting it.

Scientists working with babies as young as a few weeks old have demonstrated that our brains literally bend reality in order to create meaning. We find patterns in the dazzling world around us, and once we find them, we tend to fit new experiences into those same patterns. The patterns we make are useful, in fact necessary. Without them, we'd be adrift in an impossible ocean of bits of unrelated data. But when we organize reality in a particular way, we preclude other ways; and, we tend to cling to our schema tenaciously. This is quite useful, up to a point.

As we gain experience, we fit the details to our old schema and develop a kind of expertise in that way of looking at things. This shaping begins in the womb and continues as long as we live. The mix of our physical faculties, our family influences, our cultural context, and our personal experiences is unique for each of us, giving each of us a point of view that is unique, albeit related to our family, community, and culture. It is, quite simply, just the way we're built. It is so automatic a process, so integral a part of us, that we rarely are aware of the filters through which we see and interpret events. The filters are so embedded in us, or we in them, that we tend to assume that however we view the world is the *obvious* way to see it—the *normal* way, the way of *common sense*. That predisposes us to judging others' perspectives as *illogical* or *abnormal,* when their visions aren't the ones we see through our own lens. It takes practice to see ourselves as others see us and to see the world as others see the world.

Making the Lenses Visible by Creating Collages

Sometimes, in order to learn new concepts, we have to let go of old notions and see the world with fresh eyes. Once we are able to do that, our brains reorganize. We create new paradigms that tend to incorporate both the old and the new views. The good news is, as Oliver Wendell Holmes Jr. once said, that "man's mind stretched to a new idea never goes back to its original dimensions." Cognitively, we have grown; and in that growing, we are better able to participate as citizens of a democracy.

Through creating collages that exemplify how various filters might produce various visions of reality, we have an opportunity to explore the power of these filters to shape our vision. This serves two functions. First, it gives us a glimpse into alternative ways of seeing, broadening our possibilities, encouraging us to shift up to a new, more inclusive paradigm. Second, it lays a foundation for subsequent inquiries in which students consider what lens they wish to deliberately invite an audience to look through (see Chapter 6, Picture This, and Chapter 7, Making History).

A Note About Materials

It's important to collect a rich array of raw materials for this project. If you assign students the task of locating images, you may need to be ready to step in with some supplies to augment what they are able to find. If you do the activity within the confines of your classroom, you'll need sources to support each of the quotes you select with images. Fortunately, it's not difficult to do this. Once you know you will be doing a collage activity, you can begin to stockpile magazines of all kinds. Pay attention to the range of activities pictured in the magazines, the range of cultures, and the variety of relationships shown. Among the potential images, there should be plenty that reflect each student's own ethnic group or identity.

What Does History Look Like?

In the suggested activity in the following section, students discuss their ideas of what history is, and then are randomly assigned a quote from history. Working individually, in pairs, or in small groups, they research the quote and its author, then locate images that support that quote and arrange them in a collage. The unit can be focused on a more specific concept within the study of history as well, such as revolution, democracy, war and peace, progress, the Depression. Through their own efforts to exemplify a worldview, and through all the students sharing and discussing their collages, they can begin to critically examine the implications of our various lenses on the world.

The Steps

1. Prepare a range of quotations that answer the overall guiding question: "What is history?" or "What is revolution?" or "What is democracy?" and so forth. The quotations should be widely divergent in point of view. You might want to have one quotation for each group or individual in the class depending on how you are structuring this aspect of the project. Here are a number of quotations you may find useful:

   "History is like a story in a way: It depends on who's telling it."
   —Dorothy Salisbury Davis

   "The history of all previous societies has been the history of class struggles."—Karl Marx

   "History teaches us that men and nations behave wisely once they have exhausted all other alternatives."—Abba Eban

"History is but the biography of great men."—Thomas Carlyle

"It is sometimes very hard to tell the difference between history and the smell of skunk."—Rebecca West

"History moves in contradictory waves, not in straight lines."
—Lois Beck and Nikki Keddie

"History becomes more and more a race between education and catastrophe."—H. G. Wells

"The history of every country begins in the heart of a man or a woman."—Willa Cather

"All history is a record of the power of minorities, and of minorities of one."—Ralph Waldo Emerson

"All big changes in human history have been arrived at slowly and through many compromises."—Eleanor Roosevelt

"We are not makers of history. We are made by history."
—Martin Luther King Jr.

"Natural selection, as it has operated in human history, favors not only the clever but the murderous."—Barbara Ehrenreich

"History is a relentless master. It has no present, only the past rushing into the future. To try to hold fast is to be swept aside."
—John Fitzgerald Kennedy

"History would be a wonderful thing . . . if only it were true."
—Leo Tolstoy

"'History,' Stephen said, 'is a nightmare from which I am trying to awake.'"—James Joyce

"A people without a history is like the wind on buffalo grass."
—Crazy Horse

"History is a stern judge."—Svetlana Alliluyeva

"History is more or less bunk. It's tradition. We don't want tradition. We want to live in the present and the only history that is worth a tinker's damn is the history we make today."—Henry Ford

"History, real solemn history, I cannot be interested in. The quarrels of popes and kings, with wars and pestilences in every page; the men all so good for nothing, and hardly any women at all."
—Jane Austen

"History is a child building a sand-castle by the sea, and that child is the whole majesty of man's power in the world."—Heraclitus

"History is, indeed, little more than the register of the crimes, follies, and misfortunes of mankind."—Edward Gibbon

"That men do not learn much from the lessons of history is the most important of all the lessons that history has to teach."—Aldous Huxley

"There is no life that does not contribute to history."—Dorothy West

"People are trapped in history and history is trapped in them."—James Baldwin

"History is a vast early warning system."—Norman Cousins

"The past is always being changed."—Jorge Luis Borges

"Very often history is a means of denying the past."—Jeanette Winterson

"History does not unfold. It piles up."—Robert M. Adams

"Human history is work history. The heroes of the people are work heroes."—Meridel Le Sueur

2. Introduce the activity with a general discussion of how a person's point of view influences her or his perception of an event. If you've done the activity in Chapter 2, The History of the Class, you can ask students to remember the documents they wrote and consider how each exemplified a particular point of view from within the class. You can also discuss the notion of point of view as expressed in proverbs, quotations, and sayings: every rope has two ends; life is just a bowl of cherries; when the elephants fight, it is the grass that is trampled; a rolling stone gathers no moss; it takes a village to raise a child; one man's meat is another man's poison; and so forth. Invite students to think of other such sayings. What points of view are being expressed in the sayings? If I believe life is a bowl of cherries, how will I perceive adversity? Is it possible to avoid being trampled if I am grass and the elephants are fighting? If I am the elephant, do I even notice the grass? What are examples of one person's meat that might be another person's poison?

3. Ask students to define history (or whatever concept you are focusing on). This can be a whole-class discussion, a journal assignment, a one-line in-class writing activity followed by discussion, or a small-group or partner discussion. The main idea is to have the students commit to an idea of their own about what history is before shifting

to look at history through the lens of another. You might want to structure this as a dialogue journal, in which students work in pairs to discuss the question—"What is history?"—on paper by writing notes back and forth to each other. Then, they read each other's contributions to the discussion and circle what they think is the most memorable phrase or sentence in their partner's writing. These circled phrases or sentences can then be written on tagboard and posted around the room as Quotes of the Week. (We are indebted to Bob Tierney, a teacher leader with the Bay Area Writing Project, for this simple but effective exercise.)

4. Choose two or three very contrasting quotations from history to display on the overhead or chalkboard. Ask students to consider how the view or definition one has of history affects one's perceptions of events. For example, if you see history as "a relentless master," with "no present, only the past rushing into the future," as John Fitzgerald Kennedy characterized it, how will you interpret an event such as the announcement that a human has been cloned? How will your perception of that event differ if you see history as "a race between education and catastrophe" as did H. G. Wells? Suppose you feel, as did Karl Marx, that history is the history of "class struggles"? How could cloning be accounted for in that vision? How would each of these points of view color interpretation of the next presidential election? Choose these and/or other items that are in the news or are a part of your curriculum as examples for discussion.

5. Discuss where one's definition of history comes from. Students will hopefully cite a variety of influencing factors, including their own experiences, parental or caretaker values, the time and place they happen to live in, and so on.

6. Explain that the assignment they'll be working on next is to research a famous quotation from history to do the following:

   • Find out about the person who said it: When did she or he live? Is the person still alive? What was going on in the world when the person was alive? What did the person do that was either relevant or not relevant to the project at hand?

   Be sure that students can paraphrase, or explain accurately what the person who said the quotation meant by it, by relating the quotation to what they've found out in the preceding activity. You may want to develop a worksheet for students to use as a research guide, along the lines of the example provided in Figure 3–1.

- Find images to put into a collage that exemplify the point of view of the quote.
- Create a collage that has the quotation as its title (see example in Figure 3–2). The minimum size paper I use as the background is 11″ by 17″; time and materials permitting, I'd go up to 18″ by 24″.
- Present the collage to the class, and be able to answer questions about the life of the person and the reason for choosing the particular images that were included.

Quotation Research

Name _____ Date _____ Period _____

What quotation are you researching?

Who was the author of this quotation?

When was she or he born?   Where?

Why is this person well known to us?

What were his or her major accomplishments?

What were you able to find out about this person's beliefs, philosophy, or thinking in general?

What important events were happening in history when this person lived that might have had an effect on him or him?

What do you think this person meant in the quotation? Put it into your own words.

Where did you find out about this person?

Figure 3–1 *Quotation research worksheet.*

History is but the biography of great men. – Thomas Carlyle

Where Are All the Women?

Figure 3–2 *An example of a collage exemplifying one view of history.*

7. Give students appropriate opportunities—in class, trips to the library, or as homework—to do the research. The abilities of students to find their own resources will depend on various factors—age, access to libraries, Internet access, support outside the classroom. To facilitate learners, you might want to provide them with biographical information rather than have them do the research. You could develop a one- to two-page biographical sketch on each quoted figure that includes key information; or perhaps you can find good Internet articles and/or summaries that you can print for each of the historical figures quoted.

If you are working with students who need quite a bit of support and instruction in research skills, arrange with your school librarian to have resource materials on a cart that you can keep in the classroom. (Be sure to give this invaluable ally plenty of notice. Librarians can work miracles, but they need some time to do it!) You might also want to identify three or four good websites related to the project to suggest to students so that they can get started right. Review basic strategies and protocols for Internet searches too.

Another way to support students in this project is to schedule a class period in the library, a session in the computer lab, or both so that they have time to do their research. If they are adept at library and/or computer use, this can be a fairly efficient process. If students are novices, you will, of course, need to schedule more time and perhaps make explicit instructions about using these resources a part of your unit plan. Sometimes the more experienced computer users don't mind helping the beginners, but be careful not to overdo it. Technologically advanced students also need time to do their own research.

8. Finding images is another research aspect of this project. If the students have resources and skills to do so, this can be a homework project. You can also ask students to bring in newspapers, magazines, and other sources of images to contribute to a classroom pool of raw materials. To have a wide array of images available, you will need to have a wide array of printed materials. In addition to mass market publications and magazines, such as *People, Newsweek, Time, US News and World Report, USA Today,* and local daily and Sunday newspapers, look for trade magazines, magazines published by labor unions, *National Geographic,* foreign language magazines and newspapers, and travel brochures. This is also an opportunity for students to learn how to look for images on the Internet. Google.com, for example, has a bank of images that can be searched by a term or author name and then printed out. The Library of Congress has a wealth of images in its database. Students can also print out single copies of images from Encarta or other online encyclopedias.

If you aren't familiar with U.S. copyright law, this is an important time to review those portions of the law that affect teachers and students. Briefly, it is generally permissible for individual students to print or make single photocopies of documents and images for their own personal use. It is generally not permissible for a teacher to make classroom sets of documents or images without explicit permission from the copyright holders.

9. Give students appropriate opportunities, in class or as homework, to create the collage. If they will be doing the work in class, be sure to have posterboard and glue available as well as your stock of magazines and other good sources of images. Gathering images, arranging them, and gluing them can take as little as an hour or as much as several hours. If students are working in groups, they will need to have time to work together in class, both to plan their research and to plan their collage. If students are working individually, it may be more feasible to increase homework expectations.

10. Have students share their research and collages with the class, and display the collages around the room, maybe even in the school's lobby.

Some Considerations

When I know I am going to be teaching this lesson, I begin stockpiling magazines ahead of time. I try to make sure that there are at least a dozen images that I think are appropriate to each quote I've chosen. Assume too that there will be other quotations the people who are making the collages will find and see as relevant.

When I'm working with groups of preservice teachers, I like to do this particular activity in randomly selected groups, and I focus just on making the collage. I have one person from each group draw a slip of paper that has the quotation written on it. I choose the quotations so that they reflect the widest variety of worldviews possible. I don't want groups to select their own quotation because I want them to practice shifting their own lens out of the way. When both the groups and the quotations are randomly selected, I think there is less opportunity for people to gravitate to a quotation that requires less mental stretching.

With middle and high school students, other considerations may be more important. Students may be more interested if they are able to choose their favorite quote. If that seems to be the case, I wouldn't insist on sticking with randomly assigned quotations. The point is always to make the learning engaging, never to be so doctrinaire that students lose interest. With any of these activities, it is important to remember that this approach's underlying philosophy is to make the work engaging and relevant to the students, so I certainly don't want to turn that energy off in favor of a strict interpretation of the assignment. If you know where you're going with an activity, you can always explore some alternate routes for getting there.

Debriefing

Once the collages are finished and on display, ask students to consider questions similar to those you might use in analyzing a photograph (see Chapter 6, Picture This).

• What do you see in the picture (without judgment or interpretation)?

• What draws your eye?

• What do you feel as you look?

• What are we not being shown?

• What other kinds of images would fit into the *world* of this collage?

- What kinds of images would contradict the *world* of this collage?
- In your opinion, is this a *complete* vision of history? Why or why not?
- If this is your vision of history, how do you tend to see and/or interpret events that are in the news today?
- Taken as a group, are any of the illustrated quotations especially at odds with one another? Do any of them complement one another?

Extensions and Variations

1. We can circle back to The History of the Class exercise from Chapter 2, I, Witness to History, and have each group that has made a collage write a history of the class that expresses the lens or bias of their collage. In such a case, the group working with the Carlyle quote— "History is but the biography of great men"—might give even more attention to the obviously charismatic figure of Matthew Martinson and also make sure that the math teacher is mentioned by name. A view of the class through this lens might emphasize the personalities and teaching styles of the professors and give short shrift to the students. On the other hand, a group looking at The History of the Class through Marx-colored lenses might find a way to comment visually on class issues in the education profession, and how the program they are in either does or does not effectively address those issues. A group focusing on the race between education and catastrophe might come up with something that emphasizes the urgency of programs, such as this one, to prepare teachers to be effective educators before it is too late!

2. Students can bring in photos from newspaper accounts, without the captions. The class can then create a number of captions for the photos, reflecting some of the biases they've explored through collage, or others they've explored through class discussion. (See Chapter 2, I, Witness to History, for a more complete discussion of this option.)

3. Students can create posters that reflect their own definitions of history, and compare and contrast their own definitions with the others on display.

4. Students can write reflective journals or essays about what they perceive to be their own lenses or biases.

5. Students can examine the textbooks and other books in their classes and look for obvious and hidden bias. For a fuller discussion of this activity, see Chapter 5, The Media: Servant of (Too?) Many Masters.

6. Kristin Nichols, a teacher mentioned more extensively in Chapter 4, Trading Stories, suggests a variation on looking at the world through rose-colored glasses. Students are given sturdy paper strips, folded and shaped like eyeglasses. They are instructed to decorate the glasses and cut out the eyeholes in any pattern they like. After they've completed their glasses, they put them on. All are asked to draw a particular object or scene as they see it through their own personalized lenses. The results are compared and discussed.

7. An exercise related to number 6 is to have students take up positions at various places and from various vantage points in the classroom, and then describe what they see and hear. Some of them might be facing corners of the room, or staring up at the ceiling or down at the floor; others may have a more inclusive view. You can spice it up by adding some sound effects—a thump or a crash, a whispered unintelligible but urgent conversation, that sort of thing. The students who are facing away from the source will have only the sounds and no visual cues about what is making them. How do their descriptions of what they see and hear differ from those who have a better view? Does any one person have the whole picture of the classroom? Are there significant aspects of the classroom that are not captured at all by any of the accounts? (An astute fourth grader doing this exercise once pointed out in the class discussion that none of the descriptions included the real life of the classroom, which was all the students and the teacher, and how they learned together.)

8. Another variation of the basic collage activity is to employ it in other related contexts. For example, Seattle's Cleveland High School students who were studying labor history created collages that reflected images of labor. Wendy Ewbank, seventh-grade social studies teacher at Seattle Girls' School, wanted both to help her students make connections between the American Revolution and more contemporary events and to have them think critically about what revolution really means. She gave them a dictionary definition of revolution, along with several quotations.

First, the students were to find quotes from their social studies text and from the historical novel they'd chosen to read about the Revolutionary War era. If they couldn't find much in their books, she gave them a list of quotations from which to choose (see representative list in the chapter's Appendix). In any case, their instructions were to make a collage that reflects the sentiments of the person who said the quotation. Next, she suggested that they put the quotation

Figure 3–3 *Students select images that illustrate a particular point of view.*

into their own words; some of them included this paraphrase in their collage. They could also add words they thought of in response to the quotation. Students researched the images as homework, using the Internet, encyclopedias, magazines, and newspapers. The collage in Figure 3–3 features one of the students' favorite quotations from John F. Kennedy: "Those who make peaceful revolution impossible will make violent revolution inevitable."

Another student focused on women as revolutionaries. Her collage featured contrasting images of women. On the left were tearful women. Connecting the two sides were the words: "People think of women as 'helpless and defenseless humans,' but really they are a big part of all revolutions!" From the novel she'd read, she selected "Men must fight and women must weep, but you'll get no tears from me!" and added her own words, "For example: During the Revolutionary War, Mercy Otis Warren helped by telling people about what the loyalists were doing, and she gave a lot of speeches, and she also wrote a lot." The images on the right of the collage ranged from Joan of Arc to Rosie the Riveter to women in uniform on armed forces' recruiting posters.

9. Some students elected to do original artwork, or to mix collage images with their own artwork. One student chose, for example, to create a poster that contemplates a quote from James Fenimore Cooper's book, *The Spy*, about the ambiguity of serving one's country as a spy but dying without the public knowing the true story.

Biased for Inclusion and Complexity

By now, it is hopefully clear that when we talk of identifying our lens or bias, we are not using the term *bias* necessarily as a pejorative term. We *all* are biased. We all are born into a world in which our environment and our experiences literally shape the way we see. We couldn't function if we weren't able to select some details in our environment and ignore others. What we are hoping for is that, in the process of identifying our own lenses and in the process of training our eye to see through the lens of another, we are developing the habits of mind that will bring us to a functional appreciation of the complexity of human affairs. We need to know where we stand, but we also need to know what the journey looks like if we're walking in someone else's shoes. It is this interplay that is the foundation of democratic systems.

Resources

NCSS. 1994. *Expectations of Excellence: Curriculum Standards for Social Studies*, Bulletin 89. Silver Springs, Maryland: NCSS.

Quotations and Biography Research Websites

www.bartleby.com/100/—The combined databases of *Bartlett's Familiar Quotations, Simpson's Contemporary Quotations,* and *The Columbia World of Quotations.*
www.Biography.com—A searchable database of 25,000 biographies.
www.google.com—To search directly on this or any other search engine, enclose the entire name in quotation marks.
www.quotationspage.com/—A searchable database of more than 15,000 quotations.
www.quoteland.com/—An eclectic collection of quotes.
www.s9.com/biography—A searchable database of 28,000 biographies.

Book of Quotations

Maggio, Rosalie. 1996. *The New Beacon Book of Quotations by Women.* Boston: Beacon Press. Maggio's book contains 16,000 quotations by 2,600 women, and it provides an antidote, so to speak, to the more standard quotation collections, which tend to be heavily dominated by quotations by men.

Appendix

Quotations About Revolution

"The successful revolutionary is a statesman, the unsuccessful one a criminal."—Erich Fromm

"The most radical revolutionary will become a conservative the day after the revolution."—Hannah Arendt

"Revolution is not a dinner party, not an essay, nor a painting, nor a piece of embroidery; it cannot be advanced softly, gradually, carefully, considerately, respectfully, politely, plainly and modestly."—Mao Zedong

"The most heroic word in all languages is revolution."—Eugene V. Debs

"This country, with its institutions, belongs to the people who inhabit it. Whenever they shall grow weary of the existing government, they can exercise their constitutional right of amending it, or exercise their revolutionary right to overthrow it."—Abraham Lincoln

"When people revolt in a totalitarian society, they rise not against the wickedness of the regime but its weakness."—Eric Hoffer

"Those who make peaceful revolution impossible will make violent revolution inevitable."—John F. Kennedy

"Democracy is therefore not a revolutionary institution. On the contrary it is the very means of preventing revolution and civil wars. It provides a method for the peaceful adjustment of government to the will of the majority."—Ludwig von Mises

"Revolutionary upheavals may change how the world looks but seldom changes the way the world works. Lasting historical change comes not through tidal waves but through the irresistible creeping tide."
—Richard M. Nixon

"The evils which are endured with patience as long as they are inevitable, seem intolerable as soon as a hope can be entertained of escaping them."—Alexis de Tocqueville

"Revolution devours its own parents as well as its own children."
—Helen Foster Snow

"It is better to die on your feet than to live on your knees!"
—Dolores Ibarruri

"No real social change has ever come about without a revolution."
—Emma Goldman

"All revolutions are treason until they are accomplished."
—Amelia E. Barr

4

Trading Stories

To see a world in a grain of sand

—William Blake

uy American!" the bumper sticker on the car in front of us sternly admonishes. But what does that mean? The car that sports it is a Ford—made in Mexico. We are driving a Honda—made in Tennessee. Which is one of *ours* and which is one of *theirs*?

Surely there is nothing more American than a Barbie doll. Barbie, at least, must be ours, and her manufacturer, Mattel, is based in California. But she was originally created in Germany (modeled after a German bar girl for American soldiers). Barbie and her friends are made of plastic manufactured from Arabian oil, with hair created in Japan, pellets from Taiwan, clothing sewn in factories in China and the Philippines. Her various parts are assembled in factories in mainland China. Only then does she join the parade of millions of immigrants who have come to the shores of the United States to become *American*. At that point, she will most likely take up residence on the store shelves of a multinational corporate entity while she awaits purchase. Indeed, there are very few manufactured items that we use these days that can be said to be 100 percent *Made in the USA*.

In a consumer society like ours, many children are far removed from a sense of connection to even the most basic elements of survival. Their food appears on the table or in vending machines; their shelter is built not from stones, mud, trees, or animal skins in the neighborhood, but from lumber and

56

plasterboard and bricks produced in distant, unseen sawmills and factories.

Ironically, as the world becomes increasingly *inter*dependent and complex, a young person's perception of it may become equally disconnected and simplistic. Their clothing comes from stores in malls, separated by generations and continents from the Spinning Jenny their great, great-grandmothers might have used to make cotton or flax into thread; or from the process of trapping, skinning, tanning, and stitching that their ancestors perfected in order to have winter coats.

One of the simplest entry points to this kind of learning is through an exploration of everyday materials—the things that ordinary people use on a regular basis. It might be the clothing we wear; the cars we drive; the computers, CD players, VCRs, or televisions we use; the food we eat; or the sports equipment we shoot, kick, pass, pitch, or wear.

What can we learn about the world through an exploration of a simple, ordinary object? This approach, developed with artist–educator Don Fels, is exemplified by a project assignment, which makes clear the depth of learning that is possible.

A Product Research Project

The following three-week (or longer) project provides an opportunity for students to learn more about how the economic world of the twenty-first century operates, and how economic factors influence cultural, social, geographical, and political factors as well. Students will trace the manufacture and distribution of common, ordinary products and will discover just how complicated that trail is. They will come to an understanding of why it makes economic sense to build a factory in Sri Lanka, or the Philippines, rather than to build it down the block the way they might have fifty years ago. And why, a couple of years from now, it will make economic sense to abandon those factories in order to move to a new location and build another factory where labor costs are a little lower and the environmental standards are a little more lax.

Learning About the World Through Ordinary Things

Product research is a good subject to focus on for learning about the world for a number of reasons. First, it begins with the students. They will be researching items that they value, that they care about, that they actually wear or use. This means they are likely to be interested in the activity and invested in its outcome. Students will come to realize that people spend their work lives manufacturing the items we use, and there are significant economic, geographic, and political consequences to the economic connections that encircle the globe. They will also find out that the people who make their shoes and shirts may not experience the kinds of lives and working conditions the students wish they would.

Second, encouraging students to carry out open-ended research about the manufacturing process is an apolitical approach to what can be contentious and partisan issues. You are not asking students to uncover dirty practices or scandal, to proclaim or denounce economic systems, or to come to a particular or predetermined conclusion. You are simply asking them to find out what they can find out about the manufacturing process and the process of moving goods around the world.

Third, students are learning how to carry out research, and this is a set of skills and behaviors that will serve them throughout the rest of their lives. Fourth, students learn more about working in groups by dealing with others to carry out projects and to make presentations to others in order to share what they have learned.

Finally, the project serves as a touchstone for the rest of the year, and beyond. It encourages students to make connections, to realize that various elements of the world community are related in various ways, and to understand that those connections have consequences. This project will help students learn about the world, starting with what they are wearing, eating, kicking, and/or catching. It starts local and touches the farthest reaches of the planet, and once they see the connections, they will never look at their world the same way ever again.

More About Open-Ended Research

Open-ended research leads to an increased understanding of complex, interconnected, interrelated situations. Even that sentence is complex, but what it means is actually pretty simple. Take a look at something in the world that you are curious about—find out why it is the way it is, how it came to be that way, how it relates to the larger world in which it exists. It's what we do in the real world when we want to know something, and it is something we can help our students learn and practice.

The kind of research encouraged here is different from that often practiced in school. It is an open-ended process, so called because it is not aimed at a predetermined, *correct* answer but is in response to a real question. This means many things, including the following:

- The student may or may not find what he or she is looking for, in terms of desired information.

- Original questions may give way to other, more relevant or compelling questions as the research continues.

- There is no preset agenda that the researcher brings to the research except to find out as much as possible about a topic or product.
- There is no one, complete source for information, and a thorough search may require consulting several different kinds of resources.
- The most effective manner of *report* may only become evident after the research has been done. What the researcher decides to communicate about his or her research will have a strong bearing on the ways in which the results are communicated.

This kind of research takes patience, trial and error, and the ability to make connections and to see patterns. It takes practice, and paying attention. It offers students the opportunity to search for meaning, to ask real questions as the process continues: What have I found? What does it mean? How are the pieces related? What have I missed? Who's voice is absent or overbearing? What doesn't fit? How is this like or unlike other things I have studied? Where do I go next? In addition, there is a real need to self-monitor the research process, to check and recheck, and to make sure that you are not leaving out a point of view or a constituent who has something to say.

This is the way real people learn about things in the real world. We ask real questions and then try to figure out how to answer them as well as possible. It isn't looking up the state capitol of Washington, on page 52 of the *W* volume; it is posing a real, multifaceted question of real interest, then taking the time to find out what you can find.

This is an open-ended assignment, and as such may require some fine-tuning as it goes. You know your students, your curriculum schedule, and your resources. Make the assignment as challenging, as ongoing, and as structured (or un-) as you and your students are ready to handle. Make the presentations more structured or traditional if that fits the needs of you and your students. The bottom line is not the assignment (it never is); it is the learning of the students. Do what is right for them and for you.

Project Overview

This assignment is designed for groups of three or four students. Each group should select a product that is made somewhere outside of this country and find out as much as possible about the production and distribution of that product. Each group will make a presentation to the rest of the class. This presentation is designed to be multidimensional rather than simply written and read, though as mentioned before, do what makes the most sense for you and your students.

The Steps

There are many steps and this may seem intimidating at first, but there is nothing complicated about the process. It usually takes two to three weeks (though not every day and not always full periods) to carry out, so make sure you give yourself and your students enough time to complete it. It's well worth the time you give to the project.

1. Ask students to read the labels of their favorite items of clothing, sporting equipment, CD player, or something they use to find out what they can about where it is made. This can be done as a homework question, or in class; although as a homework assignment, it allows students to research items they have there (and to read labels from clothing they may not be able to access in a classroom). Make a list of the products on the board using the information the students have obtained from the label. Typically, the information says something like: Made in Taiwan or Manufactured in Macao or perhaps Assembled in China.

2. Form small groups. There are many ways to do this; use a method that works for you and your students. Ask each group to choose one product to research.

3. Help students generate a list of questions about their products. You might begin by having the student groups make their own lists, or you might choose to share a list of questions such as the one that follows. There are advantages to each approach. Starting with a teacher-generated list helps beginning researchers focus and provides them with some structure. Student-generated lists might take longer to compile and may not immediately lead to efficient research efforts; however, the students will learn more about research, about posing questions, and about working together. They will be able to make changes to their own lists as they perceive the need to do so, furthering their learning.

   Here is a sample list of questions in case you make that choice. Feel free to substitute your own questions, or to pick from among this list:

   • Where was your product made?

   • Where is this country located on a map? Who are its immediate neighbors?

   • What is it like there? What is the climate of the region? What grows there?

   • How do people live their lives? What are their beliefs and customs and institutions and values?

- Who owns or controls the factory where the product is produced?
- Who works in this factory? Where do they come from? How were they recruited?
- What would they be doing if they were not working in the factory? What other kinds of work possibilities are there in the place that they live?
- Who designed the product? Who is it made for?
- How does the product get from the factory to the store in which it is sold (e.g., REI, Old Navy, or The Gap)? Include in this answer as much information as you can find about the product's path.
- How much does it cost to make the product?
- How much does it cost to buy the product?
- How much do the people who make the product get paid?
- Where would the product have been made 100 years ago?
- What do the factory workers wear in their everyday lives and where do those clothes come from? This question is most appropriate if the students are researching an item of clothing (e.g., what kinds of shoes are they wearing while they manufacture Nike sneakers).
- Why was the product made overseas rather than near to the place it is sold?
- What is the connection between the local store and the factory: Do they own it or contract with a local owner, or are there some other arrangements?
- What impact has the factory had on the area in which it exists?
- What is your research trail? What did you try and where would you go next if you had more time? (This step must be included in the report.)

5. Brainstorm a list of possible sources of information about the product. Where might you go to learn more about the place the product is made, about the people who make the product, and about the process involved in making and delivering the product? (A potential list of sources is included later in this activity.) Assist students as needed based on their skill levels, knowledge, and experience. You want them to grow and learn (don't give them all the answers), but you don't want them to be overwhelmed or too frustrated such that they get nowhere and give up. Have the students post their research discoveries (good sources of information) in a public part of the room so that all can benefit from their finds.

6. Create a timeline for the project. It is important for you to set check-points along the way so that you (and the students) can monitor how groups are proceeding and problem solve whenever necessary. Set up library time, either in the school library or at the public library (or both). Make contact with the librarians because they may be able to gather books on the topic, if given enough lead-time, so that you can make good use of your time there. Some libraries will also allow you to check out large numbers of books to the classroom so that you can do research at home. Reserve time in the school computer lab if you have Internet access.

   Note: Make sure to allow sufficient time for research responses, espe-cially to inquiries via email or letter, which may take some time. Many companies have local offices and toll-free numbers to their corporate headquarters should you need to make calls there. Otherwise, more and more contact is able to be made through websites, which offer the possibility, though not the certainty, of a quick response.

7. This is an opportunity to teach and practice research skills. The following are several related and relevant skills for this task:
   - How does reading nonfiction differ from reading fiction?
   - How do you evaluate information?
   - How do you deal with conflicting information?
   - How do you recognize the role of bias and point of view in what you are finding in print, on the Internet, through interviews?
   - How do you know what to write down and what to let go so that you don't end up copying everything?
   - How do you know when you have enough information?
   - How do you keep track of your information and sources so that you (or someone else) can find them again?
   - How do you conduct an interview?
   - How do you recognize your own bias or point of view? What role might that play in your research efforts?
   - How do you make sure all voices and points of view are included?
   - How do you make sure that you are not simply getting company or official policy?

   It makes sense to practice these skills (those you choose to focus on) as a whole group. It is best to have students practice the desired skill with material that is simple enough (content- and readingwise) so that the sole challenge is the new skill to be learned. Once they are comfortable with the new skill, they will then be able to apply it to their particular research process as a next step.

8. Divide the work so that everyone is involved. Take advantage of skills and interests within each group so that the students are building on their strengths, and also learning new skills.

9. Conduct check-in meetings with each group. It's a chance to ask the group what they've found, and for you to assess whether they are making progress. You can also help them to make sense of what they are finding. For example, one group kept running into dead-ends while researching Nike, and they decided to identify those dead-ends as information—Nike is not willing to answer our questions—that got included in their presentation. You can help group members decide what more they need to find out, and help them develop a plan for doing so. Review the students' research trail with them at this time, both to remind them that they should have one (in writing), because it will help you and them discover possible gaps in their research strategy to date, and to suggest possible future research steps they might take.

10. Students then carry out additional research based on the check-in meeting. What does the group still need to do?

11. Then the groups plan a presentation for the rest of the class. Guiding questions include: What will you share about what you have found? How is it best for you to share it? The following are several presentation models you might choose:

   • Skits and role-plays

   • Maps

   • Collages, posters, paintings

   • Music

   • Brief lecture-style presentations

   • Audience involvement

   • Models representing the product or process

   • Videodocumentary

   • Some combination of approaches

   Remind students that they and their classmates will be sitting through several of these presentations. What can they do to help their audience stay interested and learn about the product from them?

12. Help the students to decide what they need in order to make their presentation, and to strategize how they will get those items.

13. Make sure a written research trail is included with each group's materials, documenting where they found information and how one could locate it again.

14. Students should evaluate their group process. How did it go? What would they do differently? How did each of them help his or her group carry out the task? What did he or she learn about the product? Were they successful in helping each other to learn? How do they know that?

15. Consider taking social action. What have we learned, and are there related public steps we might want to take in response to what we have found? Could we carry out education campaigns to let others know about the situation? Write letters to newspapers, or to the local school district, if what students have found has possible implications for district policy (like deciding not to buy products from companies who are operating sweatshops, for example).

16. Pulling it all together. How was what the class groups found out different and how was it similar? What are common issues and what is unique to each industry? How might the class share this information, or communicate about it with others? How does it relate to other issues we have studied in U.S. history, in state history, or elsewhere? How are the lives of the workers similar or different to those of workers in the United States, in our hometown, or related to those of us in this classroom? How have things changed over time in our own community? We can investigate the last question in terms of the types of work that people do, the working conditions at their job sites, the people who are in the labor force (race, gender, age), and the consequences that arise from those changes.

Where to Look for Information

One of the major challenges to succeeding in this project is to make sure that the students can find enough information about their product. This is more possible than you (and your students) might think at first. There are several major sources of information for a project like this, including people you or your students already know; school and public libraries; the Internet (see some useful websites listed at the end of this chapter); the port authority (in coastal cities); warehouses connected to trucking, the railroads, or airports in inland locations; local or federal government records; people who work in the store in which the item was purchased; and industry journals and magazines.

It is a very good idea to actually try this process out yourself before introducing the project so that you will be familiar with potential pitfalls and possible points of frustration for your students. Problem solve what you can ahead of time so that you can be of use to the groups as they run up against seeming dead-ends. Finally, remember that the presentation at the end is not the real objective of the lesson. We want students to learn as much as they can about open-ended research, about the production and shipping of products around the world, and about the interdependence of the world's economic system. Your students will find what they are able to find, and they shouldn't get too stressed over not finding enough information about their product.

The following is a list of possible resources that I share with my students when they start on this assignment in Seattle, Washington. Obviously, you will want to modify the list to fit available local and Internet resources.

SAMPLE RESOURCES

- People who have lived in the countries in which the products are produced, including family members, family friends, people who work with parents or guardians, or members of the school community
- Jackson School at the University of Washington. This division of the university is dedicated to outreach to the public, and features departments related to various regions of the world—for example, SE Asia, East Asia, Africa, Russia, Eastern Europe
- Port of Seattle and Tacoma (inland locations might look to railway, airport, or trucking warehouses or shipping yards)
- The Seattle Public Library's business section
- University of Washington Library
- Seattle sister city office: Seattle has more than twenty sister city connections around the world—for example, Kobe, Japan; Bergen, Norway; Haiphong, Vietnam
- S.C.O.R.E.—operated by the small business administration, staffed by volunteers who are retired from the business community; located in the Federal building in downtown Seattle
- Books and magazines
- Films—It can be a challenge to sort out what is accurate and what is receiving the Hollywood treatment, but the location shots can give information about the geography, housing, and climate
- Forums and lectures

- City or county agencies
- Cultural centers and cultural organizations
- Company websites and home offices, many of which have toll-free numbers
- Websites that are related to the product, topic, or theme—for example, coffee-industry magazines and organizations
- Related union websites, newsletters, journals, and individuals
- People who work at the store in which the product is sold— salespeople, buyers, managers, truckdrivers, or the company president may have information to share about the path your item has taken; however, it may turn out that no one at that store knows anything ...

Product Research Reports

Sample From a Fourth/Fifth-Grade Classroom

During the World Trade Organization meetings and demonstrations in Seattle during November–December 1999, my fourth- and fifth-grade students got very interested in the reasons for the meetings and the protests. I had been at the demonstrations the previous day, so we compared my experience with what the students saw on television. We spoke in general terms about the issues and concerns of the demonstrators, including child labor, environmental degradation, decision making (and the impact of WTO on democracy), genetic engineering, and genetically modified foods. While this product research unit was created and designed for secondary classes, it is adaptable, with adequate support, for younger students. I worked with my class to engage in a modified product research project.

We decided to find out what we could about a product used at school. Many of the students play soccer, so we chose soccer balls. Because this was our first try at open-ended research, and because the students are nine- to ten-year-olds, we researched this as a class rather than in small groups. When we began researching the production of soccer balls, the search quickly brought us to several pieces of information, which were gathered in a few afternoons by a team of students:

- A great majority of soccer balls are produced in Pakistan, in and around the town of Sialkot.
- About 10,000 urban workers and 30,000 rural workers are involved in making soccer balls.
- ILO (International Labor Organization) estimates as many as 7,000 Pakistani children between 5 and 14 handstitch soccer balls, working at

least 8 hours a day to make about 50 cents per ball; each completes maybe two balls a day.

- Only 22 to 25 percent of the Pakistani children go to school.
- The balls are sewn by hand.
- Child labor is a major component of the soccer ball industry.
- There are labor organizations working to change the policy of child labor. Companies, such as Nike, Reebok, and others, are both complicit in the child labor practices, and now committed to changing that policy, at least according to their public statements.
- There is a subcontractor who delivers soccer ball kits to workers in villages. The children and other workers then stitch the balls and return them to the subcontractor, who in turn returns the soccer balls to contractors (often foreign-owned) who make the balls for U.S. (and worldwide) sales.
- Soccer balls are made from synthetic leather.
- Soccer balls are made of several layers of material, usually polyester or cotton. The more layers there are, the better the soccer ball.
- Soccer balls are not all the same size.

The team then chose to communicate about the child labor issue to other students and the adults in the school community, to let the gym teacher know that child laborers might well make the soccer balls they were using. Several students also approached their soccer coaches (outside of school) expressing their concerns.

We found Pakistan on a map and located some pictures of the country to find out a little about what life would be like there. We learned about other child labor issues in Pakistan, including the story of Iqbal Masih—a Pakistani child who had been enslaved in the rug-making industry since age four. He managed to escape and traveled around the world telling about his experiences until he was murdered at age twelve.

The students were very excited to discover Craig Kielburger, a then twelve-year-old student in Toronto, Canada (he's now college age), who read about Iqbal and decided to find out about child labor for himself. He traveled around the world to see the situation firsthand, and then began an organization of fellow students who were determined to stop the practice of child labor worldwide. To date, Free the Children has built more than 250 schools for poor children around the world, and the organization has worked tirelessly to get cities and towns to commit to refusing to allow the sale of any product manufactured using child labor.

The students took inspiration from Mr. Kielburger, only slightly older than themselves, and took on social action projects in our community. For example, they decided that the dirt field and ratty playground next to our school was a problem. The park had graffiti everywhere and a field was just dirt, which means mud during most of the school year in Seattle. There was garbage everywhere and no lights, so it was a very unpleasant place to play. The students, with the help of an architect, prepared a presentation for the Seattle City Council, complete with photographs and essays; the city responded. There is now a grass field in place next to the school.

The research from this particular product (soccer balls) also leads back to the major current events of our day. The United States concluded its bombing runs over Afghanistan and then threatened to take the so-called War on Terrorism to other countries; Iraq, Iran, and North Korea were identified as the "axis of evil" by the President, and Pakistan has been mentioned as well. Well, Afghanistan is right next door to Pakistan, and the Pashtuns (among others) are a significant portion of the population in both nations. Early in the twenty-first century, Pakistan and India were lined up at their common border threatening war. So, we have to wonder, What will happen to those children who make the soccer balls we kick and throw should U.S. leaders decide to bomb there next, or if war breaks out between India and Pakistan?

Three Middle School Classrooms

Three middle school classes at Summit K–12 in Seattle took on this project in the fall of 2002, with certain modifications. They structured an assignment that would require teams of students to research either clothing or products manufactured in countries outside of the United States and were sold in Seattle stores, as described in this chapter. The teachers adapted the assignment to focus on three specific student projects. Each student team was responsible for creating a posterboard featuring photographs, facts, and other information concerning the product being researched. The teams also were required to create and present a skit highlighting a point of conflict or tension related to the manufacture of the product. Then, they had to write and perform a forty-five second commercial about the product. *Note:* The teachers chose these three activities from the long list of project options presented earlier in this chapter. They could have chosen others (and so can you).

As a follow-up, the classes carried out various social action steps, on individual, small-group, and whole-class levels, which are described later in the chapter. The teams also prepared a three-class display for the lobby of the school.

The project lasted for approximately three weeks in the classrooms at Summit. They could have gone on longer, and all three teachers are clear that they will return to the project often during the school year as they encounter other countries and issues in geography, Washington State History, and Current Events classes.

Structure

The teachers offered their students a number of structural supports along the way. The group Learning Guidelines Information Sheet helped the students to organize themselves and to develop a plan for their product research project (see Appendix A at the end of this chapter).

The teachers grouped the long list of possible guiding questions into four categories: (1) questions about the country, (2) questions about the factory, (3) questions about the lives of the factory workers, and (4) questions about the product. Each student in a group was to cover one set of questions as his or her contribution to the group. The group as a whole was responsible for presenting their research trail, including what they tried and how it worked (see Appendix A). The groups worked together, gathering information and preparing their presentations, for approximately two weeks.

Posterboards

The students' first assignment was to communicate what they found through display boards like the one shown in Figure 4–1. Teachers prepared guidelines and rubrics as they began their work. Emphasis was placed on presenting

Figure 4–1 *Students create display boards to communicate what they've discovered through research.*

boards that were visually appealing, that were effective at communicating factual information, and that were able to communicate an overview of what the researchers found. We have included copies of scoring guides, student feedback guidelines, and a sample project calendar in this chapter's Appendix B.

The Skit

The students were to create a skit that demonstrated areas of both tension and conflict related to the manufacture of their product, but also were to present factual information about the situation. The teachers emphasized, through their scoring rubric, that the students should concentrate on three main areas: communicating facts and information, highlighting areas of tension and conflict related to the manufacture of the product, and involving all members of the group in creating and performing an effective skit (see scoring guide in Appendix B).

Commercials

The third task involved having students create forty-five second commercials for products. The teachers required that commercials contain only factual information and that all of the group members be involved in both the production of and the performance of commercials (see scoring guide in Appendix B).

Presentations

Each of the three classes handled the group presentations differently. Jo Cripps' class began the project first, "blazing trail" for the other classes. Each group of students in her classes offered all three of their requirements at one time: They would present their display boards, then perform their skit, then close with their commercials. The presentations were spread out over three or four days.

Kristin Nichols' and Gail Powers' classes began a week or two after Jo's class and learned from that first group. Jo's students actually came in to advise the other two classes, and modeled their boards, skits, and commercials for the students. As a result, Kristin's and Gail's students presented their display boards, and wrote scripts for their skits and commercials without actually performing them (due to time constraints).

Teacher Observations and Comments

After completing the unit with their students, the teachers made the following observations—excerpts from conversations with Jo Cripps (JC), Kristin Nichols (KN), and Gail Powers (GP):

1. (KN) The most powerful learning (I think, in retrospect) was the

discussions we had after the presentations. The students had carried out the research, had some knowledge and some questions, and we could discuss what they had found and presented with real knowledge and informed questions. Questions after the presentations got the kids thinking. They'd done the work and now were open to thinking and listening. The kids were relaxed after completing their presentations and lots of information came spilling out. They could talk about what they understood.

2. (All three) This project offers a great opportunity for kids of all skill levels. You couldn't tell which were the IEP (special education) students or who had really low skills. Many students were really very highly skilled in areas such as research or designing boards, or in oral presentation. They were able to succeed in ways that they normally could not with a traditional, book-centered curriculum. They often surprised their team members with how well they performed.

    Kristin related a story about one student who is a young man diagnosed with severe ADHD and also fetal alcohol effect. He stayed involved and kept working throughout the project, worked responsibly and effectively as a member of his team, kept looking for new information, and performed way beyond what we had ever seen from him. When his grandmother came in for her family–school conference, she saw the project boards and said, "Oh, now I know what he was talking about." He had been telling her he didn't want to buy Nike shoes anymore and she was not sure why. The project had reached him and he had taken it into his life.

3. (All three) It is crucial to allow sufficient time for the students to develop and practice group skills. This is especially true if this sequence is carried out at the beginning of the year. Group skills don't just happen. You have to teach them and give the students a chance to practice them, to problem solve when things don't work out as well as they might. Do not assume the students will be able to get together outside of class. We needed to make sure that we allocated enough in-class time for the students to complete their work. All three teachers encouraged their students to meet outside of class but it wasn't realistic for many of them.

4. (JC) It was useful to have assigned roles within the groups (archivist, designer, researcher, reporter), to have structure to support the students as they began their work. They sometimes changed roles, or had those roles overlap, but the structure helped them organize their efforts.

5. (All three) We will refer to this project throughout the rest of the year. It is a wonderful introduction to people in other places and to the people who live in them. What is it like in other places, especially those we don't know much about? How is it similar to and how is it different from the life we know about? What is the connection between the geography of the place and the ways people live, the ways they make their livings, and the ways they relate to the rest of the world? We ask questions about work, about the lives of people and the relationships of their lives and their work in every area we study. The project serves as a touchstone for all of the work we do during the rest of the year, and brings economics into our discussions of geography and history, which is unusual.

6. (KN) The posterboards remain up around the room, which is great for the kids. When someone comes into the room, their attention is usually grabbed by the posters and they gravitate toward them. One of the kids will inevitably jump up and offer a mini-tour of the boards and the project, talking with the visitor about what they did and what they learned.

   The kids also posted valuable resources they had found on the board, and these became common resources for the entire class. There was real excitement across the whole room when a group shared a particularly valuable website they had found, and this sharing really helped build the classroom community.

7. (All three) The research makes it clear to the students why what happens in other places does matter to us in the United States. The issue of interdependence—the ways in which we depend on each other around the world—is clearly brought out. Why can we have bananas and coffee in the morning, in Seattle, in December? What does that mean, and how does that happen? We talked about that in class.

8. (KN and GP) The teachers staggered the project across the three classes, with one class going first. This meant that the other two classes could benefit from the experiences of the first class. Students from the first class were able to coach fellow students from the second two classes, which meant that those students had to organize their knowledge and figure out how to *teach* it—a great teaching tool. They said things like, "It's hard and you can do it. Here's what we found was useful . . . , and here are some dead-ends that we found that maybe you can avoid." And, "This resource is really cool!"

9. (KN and GP) Give visual models of what the posters should look like, or at least what is expected so that there is a clear target. It was very important for the students to have a clear picture of what the target was, of what was expected, and both of us found it very helpful when Jo's students came in to share their completed posterboards. (None of the teachers wanted to present such a strong example that it would certainly be copied, but the students needed to know what they were aiming for with their projects.)

10. (All three) There are some groups that will struggle with this project. Make sure there are ways to support those students, either within the class structure or outside of it. We used instructional assistants to spend extra time with certain students and groups, and it was important to do so. Also know that some students may not successfully complete the project, but they can still learn from the work of their classmates and from their own efforts.

11. (All three) Parents have said that their students' thinking has changed as a result of this project. They are going through the house looking at labels, and looking at labels as they shop. Even those who are buying the same products (sneakers, for example) are not doing so thoughtlessly. All agree that it has changed the way they look at the world, and changed the conversations they have at school. The Summit classes will be sharing what they have learned from the product research project with the rest of the school via a displaycase presentation, featuring their posterboards and explanations of what they did and what they discovered.

Follow-up Projects

Summit Classes' Projects

The students in Kristin's class took what they have learned and shaped it into newspaper articles and editorials. They were studying the various forms of writing that appear in newspapers, and working to understand the ways in which newspapers are put together; this project offered them content to use. Some played with the notion of writing from a U.S. point of view while others wrote from *within* the country in which the various manufacturing efforts were actually carried out, exploring the notions of context and point of view and how these affect the stories we read and write. We've included a sample of student stories in Chapter 5.

Students in all three classes read and responded to an article that appeared in *The Nation* magazine—"The Shame of Meatpacking" by Karen Olsson (16 September 2002, pp 11–15). The assignment read as follows:

Assignment: You are to read the article and write a reflection paper. Please think of the following questions:

- How do the issues that the meatpackers face compare to the issues in your PRP factory? What are the similarities and differences?
- Explain the role of unions in the meatpacking industry. How do they influence change?
- What changes might we see if unions were allowed in your PRP factory?
- What personal reactions do you have to this article?

Form: Minimum one-page reflection, typed, due December 9

Jo's class joined the National Labor Committee for Worker and Human Rights list (see *www.nlcnet.org*) and became involved in an ongoing letter-writing campaign aimed at the Disney Corporation. The campaign urges Disney to return to a factory they had abandoned when workers demanded better pay and working conditions. Jo's students sent letters to Michael Eisner, the CEO at Disney, urging him to "do the right thing," and to respect the rights of those women who manufacture Disney products. A sample letter is shown in Figure 4–2.

A School Display

The three classes are planning to offer a visual display/report about their research projects and findings to the rest of the school. They will organize their posterboard presentations, newspaper articles, letters, and other work into a display that will be featured in the school's main floor display case, visible to the entire student community and to visitors. They felt it was important to share what they had found with others, and this seemed an effective way to do that.

Extensions

Connecting to Language Arts—A Day in the Life

This lesson, described briefly in *Social Studies at the Center* (Lindquist/Selwyn 2000), builds on the research done in tracing the pathway of different products. The instructions for the assignment are very simple: Students are to write a story about someone who lives in the town in which their product is manufactured. They are to tell the story of a person in this location during a typical day:

- What is their home like, and who lives in it?
- What might they do at the beginning of their day?

- What will they see, hear, smell as they walk (or bike, or drive) down the street?
- What foods will they eat?
- What games or amusements will they find?
- Will they spend any time relaxing?
- What work will they do during the day?
- What will they do after work?

December 13, 2002

Mr. Michael Eisner
Chief Executive Officer
Walt Disney Company
500 South Buena Vista Street
Burbank, California 91521

Dear Mr. Eisner,

My name is Dharma S. I go to Summit, a school in Seattle. Our class has been studying up on sweatshops, and companies like Disney. You probably already knew that what you do is sometimes wrong, but since you haven't changed you need to be told again.

I'm twelve, I'm only in the seventh grade, I already can tell right from wrong. What you do is wrong. I am talking about the Shah Makhdum factory and how you pulled out just when they decided to respect human rights. Yeah, surprise, they're humans too.

What I want to know is how you can do that to people and still respect yourself. Sure you've got money and cars but what about self-respect? Money can't do that for you. I'm not all religious but the Bible says some stuff that makes sense, like treat others how you would like to be treated. You should try it.

I got on the Internet and checked out a couple sites about sweatshops. Your name came up a lot. What you did to the Shah Makhdum factory was dirty. Can't you bear to treat humans like humans? People care a lot about what you do, maybe if you change others will follow your example. Set the standard.

Mr. Eisner, I ask you to do the the right thing. You know what it is. Reemploy the Shah Makhdum factory. The people will love you for it, and you will respect yourself for it. Think it all over.

Dharma S.

Figure 4–2 *Inquiry leads to action.*

Students can base their character on a real person, or they may entirely make up a person. Clearly, they will have to imagine some things about their character, though it should be based on as much information as they can find about the place in which their product is made. The story should be no more than three pages in length, and students should not worry about creating a riveting, exciting script. Their task is to help us to get a feel for the place so that we would recognize it should we arrive there.

The following are some handy hints for carrying out this assignment:

Read a number of picture books that take place in distant locations. Ask the students the kinds of things that the author and illustrator had to know in order to write the book. *The Day of Ahmed's Secret* (Heide/Gilliland 1990) is a wonderful example of such a book. It is a gentle and unspectacular story of a boy's day in Cairo, and carries with it a great deal of information about the city, and about the culture of at least some of the people who live in that great city.

Have the students prepare an hourly chart to serve as an outline. They can mark their character's day hour by hour and make brief notes about what he or she might be doing at that hour. They can fill in the chart and then decide what to write about to give us the best picture. If they are at work for eight hours, students don't have to give us an hour-by-hour account of their time in the factory.

Students can practice on themselves by keeping a log of what they do during the day, seeing if they can tell someone about their day. This exercise is actually interesting and useful for the students so that they see where their time actually goes.

Have the students ground their writing in the senses. Tell us what the character might see, hear, smell, taste, touch as he or she moves through the day. Who might they see? What might they hear as they step out of their house or apartment? What would they smell cooking at home or next door? What kinds of clothes would they be wearing or see on others?

Have the students share their stories and enjoy them.

Who Are We in Our Community?

One set of extensions to this assignment has at its heart the community in which you are teaching. Students can research the kinds of questions they asked about the communities in which their product is manufactured. What kinds of work do our parents and/or guardians do? What kinds of work goes on in our community? Where does our food come from? Where do our housing materials come from? What kinds of jobs were needed at the time of our grandparents or great-grandparents, and who did them and what was that like? How are the same jobs handled today? Are there some jobs that have no equivalent today, like the iceman who delivered to families before refrigerators became common? How did our families come to this community, and what role did jobs play in those moves? How have the communities in which we live changed as the economic health of the communities changed? What do children in your town do on a typical day? What do children in the various towns you researched do on a typical day?

A Note of Caution: Know that this question (and any questions that involve families) could be difficult or embarrassing to some students. For a variety of reasons, a few students and/or families may not want to share anything about their lives; perhaps a child is homeless and doesn't want classmates to know. There may be family issues or problems that they'd rather keep quiet, and families who simply prefer privacy. Respect that, and help them find other, related research tasks to carry out.

Does the Community Manufacture Something to Send Elsewhere?

A potent variation of this lesson simply reverses the direction of your exploration. You and your students investigate a product that is made locally and shipped somewhere else in the world. What can you and your students learn about the process, up to and including learning about the people and place(s) that import the product? The same range of questions would be appropriate, with a local focus, for example, linking the local climate to the materials used in assembling the product in question.

The product you investigate is, of course, absolutely dependent on what happens in your town. It's probably not the best idea to look to something as large and diverse as Microsoft products (a local company in the Puget Sound area) or a Boeing airplane because it's too complicated. Take something relatively straightforward and small enough to be manageable as a research topic (though if you and your students want to take on Boeing, have at it).

Fewer and fewer items are manufactured in the United States, and there may be some locations that no longer manufacture anything. Another option for this assignment can be to investigate the manufacturing history of your own town. Identify a now-vacant factory building and investigate what used to be manufactured there. Use the same set of questions, adapted slightly to be historically appropriate. The further work might be to explore the reasons for the town losing the factory, and the impact that loss has had on the community.

Detroit is an example of a city that has been devastated by the loss of manufacturing businesses. Once known as the Motor City, there are now fewer than 5,000 manufacturing jobs in Detroit's entire metropolitan area. The big three car companies have even moved their headquarters outside of the city limits, and no major plants are still in operation. Detroit is now a virtual ghost town from an economic point of view, with no major chain stores within the city limits. The blue-collar economy that was the backbone of the city is all but gone.

Trace the same sequence through history. Assume that you and your students have just researched the current pathway bringing Barbie and Ken dolls to the United States from their points of manufacturing overseas. What could you learn next about the manufacture of dolls fifty years ago, or one hundred years ago? Did they exist? What were they made of and where did those materials come from? Who designed and owned the production? Who made the dolls, and how did they get to market (were they in a market)? How much did they cost, and how much did they cost to produce? Who owned them and who played with them?

You are basically asking the same sequence of questions as in the original assignment, recognizing that the question—"How will they be made fifty years from now?"—is the question you answered in the original assignment. You can go back one hundred years or one thousand, for that matter, if appropriate.

What Do We Eat and How Does It Get Here?

Another category of related assignments centers on food. Students can trace the path an item of food, from the field, plantation, woods, or stream to their kitchen. The same general frame, or outline of guiding questions, presented earlier in this chapter applies to this assignment. Use the following list as a starting point for a food project.

- Where is the food item grown?
- What is the climate and geography of this location?
- Who grows the food? What is involved in that process?
- How have conditions changed (or not) in this process over the years? Who owns the process?
- If the food is grown on plantations, who owns the land? When did that happen? What happened to those who used to own the land?
- What are the lives like for those who grow the food?
- How does the food get from the growing site to the United States? How is the food transported and kept from rotting?
- How does it get from the port of entry to your town, store, and kitchen?

- What does it cost to grow the product? How much do the workers make?
- What does the product sell for in the store? How much is profit?
- Where did we buy the food fifty years ago, or did we buy the food at that time?
- What technologies have come into play?
- What environmental issues are associated with the growing of the food?
- Have there been land use issues around this crop: people forced off land, etc.?

The youngest students do not need to deal in the politics, sociology, and geopolitical complications of the food production process; they can simply find where their breakfast foods come from and, generally, how they get to their kitchens.

Older students can take on the more complex issues surrounding food, from land use to environmental concerns, to the use of the military to maintain plantations and profit in Nicaragua (or Hawaii . . .) over the past 100 years. There are also issues of immigration, population shifts, soil erosion, cultural and social consequences of this major change in the local economy and society. What happened when the different cultural, ethnic, and racial groups came together? How have those changes come down to us today?

A Local Variation
A local investigation can involve having younger students simply trace a local food from the fields (or streams) to the local market. The class can travel to a farm (if you have one) and see what the crop looks like in the field, then find it in local markets. (I'm not including cows to hamburger in this, though you could.)

Jake's Conscience
Kristin Nichols had an interaction with one of her students that exemplifies what we hope will happen.

> About four or five days after starting the Product Research Project, Jake, a leader in my class in both citizenship and academics, looked disengaged and not productive in the product research. I took him aside and asked him why he wasn't helping his team with the research. He responded, "Kristin, don't take this personally, but this just isn't very exciting." Jake continued to explain that "learning about geography and how things are made just doesn't interest me very much."

> My response to Jake (with a smile on my face) was, "Jake, it is time that you developed a social conscience."

His response *(with half of a smile)* was, "I have a regular conscience, isn't that good enough?"

"No, Jake, at fourteen years old, you need to start developing a strong social conscience." Jake just shook his head, grinned at me, and headed off to his group to work.

A few days later, when I saw Jake on his way down the hall, I asked him how his social conscience was coming along. He became excited and told me that his father had taken him out to buy new basketball shoes and that he spent most of the time looking at the labels: "I kept thinking about where the shoes were made and who was making them."

"Did you buy the shoes?" I asked him.

"I had no choice. I couldn't find anything that wasn't made somewhere else," responded Jake.

Not much else was said about Jake's developing conscience until the last week of the project when Jake came barreling through the doorway and started wagging his finger at me, accusing me of "messing with his mind." He proceeded to tell me that he had gone home and looked through all of his clothes and shoes to see where they were made. I smiled at him and said, "Congratulations, you are starting to develop a social conscience!" He smiled back and said, "Thanks."

Jake continued with the project and led his team to producing an informative project on Fubu shoes made in China.

Resources

Colman, Penny. 1994. *Mother Jones and the March of the Mill Children.* Millbrook, CT: Millbrook Press.

Heide, Florence Parry, and Judith Heide Gilliland. 1990. *The Day of Ahmed's Secret.* New York: Scholastic.

Hoose, Phillip. 2001. *We Were There, Too! Young People in U.S. History.* New York: Melanie Kroupa Books.

Linquist, Tarry, and Douglas Selwyn. 2000. *Social Studies at the Center.* Portsmouth, NH: Heinemann.

Littlefield, Holly. 1996. *Fire at the Triangle Factory.* Minneapolis: Carolrhoda Books.

Newman, Shirlee. 2000. *Child Slavery in Modern Times.* New York: Franklin Watts.

Nye, Naomi Shihab. 1995. *The Tree Is Older Than You Are. A Bilingual Gathering of Poems and Stories From Mexico with Paintings by Mexican Artists.* New York: Aladdin Paperbacks, 1995.

Olsson, Karen. 2002. "The Shame of Meatpacking," *The Nation* 16 September, 11–15.

Parker, David, with Lee Engfer and Robert Conrow. 1998. *Stolen Dreams: Portraits of Working Children.* Minneapolis: Lerner Publications.

Resource Center of the Americas. 1993. *Central American Children Speak: Our Lives and Our Dreams.* Minneapolis: Author.
Saller, Carol. 1998. *Working Children: Picture the American Past.* Minneapolis: Carolrhoda Books.

Websites

www.childlabor.org/links/—Extensive links to various websites dealing with child labor.
www.freethechildren.org—Organization started by Craig Kielburger that organizes children to work for children's rights around the world
www.maquilasolidarity.org/campaigns/nike/notmachinespr.htm—"We Are Not Machines"
www.nlcnet.org/resources/wages.htm—Apparel wage pricing sheet
www.nlcnet.org—The National Labor Committee for Worker and Human Rights
www.north-coast-xpress.com/~doretk/Issues/00-06%20SUM/madein.html—Made in USA Sweatshops
www.transnationale.org/anglais/enquetes/enquete2.htm—Sweet Honey in the Rock's song, "Are My Hands Clean"

Videos

Maria, Rage Against the Machine song/video about a young woman who works in a Maquila, a factory in Mexico where workers, often under deplorable working conditions, manufacture and assemble goods for export.
Mickey Mouse Goes to Haiti. National Labor Committee. Crowing Rooster Arts (distributor) *www.crowingrooster.org.*
One Child's Labor. 1996, April. CBS, *60 Minutes*—Segment featuring an interview with Craig Kielburger, founder of Free the Children (available from CBS Store, 1-800-542-5621).
When Children Do the Work. 1996. Produced by California Working Group—Borrows key segments from the National Labor Committee's video, *Zoned for Slavery,* and an episode of the PBS series *Rights and Wrongs.*
Zoned for Slavery. National Labor Committee (212)242–3200—Also produced by Crowing Rooster Arts. Widely available.

Appendix A

Learning Guidelines/Information Sheet

Group Information Sheet
- Our group members
- Our product
- Our reasons for choosing it
- Our game plan (at least seven specific steps)
- Three important due dates along the way

Guiding Questions
You should come up with six questions to be answered, in written form, as part of your group's presentation.

THE COUNTRY

- In what country was your product made?
- Where is this country located? What is its absolute location? Its relative location?
- What is it like in this country? What is the climate of the region? What grows there?

THE PEOPLE

- How do people live their lives in the country where your product is made?
- What are their beliefs? Their customs? Their values?
- How do these people govern themselves?
- What is their economy like?

THE FACTORY

- Who owns the factory where the product is made?
- Who manages the factory?
- What impact has the factory had on the place where it exists?

THE FACTORY WORKERS

- Who works in the factory?
- Where do the workers come from?
- How did they get their jobs?
- What is their job like? Describe their workday.
- If they weren't working in this factory, how would they be earning a living?
- What other jobs are available where they live?
- How much do the people get paid for their work at the factory? At other jobs that are available?

THE PRODUCT

- Who designed it?
- Who is expected to buy it?
- How much does it cost to make the product?
- How does the product get from the factory to the place where it is sold? (Get as much information as you can about the product's journey from source to store.)
- Where would the product have been made 100 years ago?
- Why was the product made far away from the place where it's sold?
- What is the connection between the store where the item is sold and the factory where it is made? Does the store own the factory or is there some other arrangement?

THE RESEARCH TRAIL

- Explain the steps you took to gather information. Phone calls? Interviews?
- What source(s) did you try that did not pan out?
- What unexpected source(s) did you find along the way?
- Be sure to include a formal bibliography.

Appendix B

Rubrics for Research Projects

Product Report Project Poster Scoring Guide

CRITERIA FOR EVALUATION

Each category is worth 0–5 points

____ The topic—the product! Is obvious at first glance; well portrayed

____ Poster contains at least 7 relevant and fascinating facts about the *product*

____ Contains at least 7 relevant and fascinating facts about the *country*

____ Contains at least 7 relevant and fascinating facts about the *factory*

____ Contains at least 7 relevant and fascinating facts about the *workers*

____ Contains an accurate and attractive map showing the product's *global* journey

____ Is at least 36-by-48 inches (standard Product Display Board dimensions)

____ Contains at least one relevant, detailed, and attractive diagram

____ All illustrations are thoroughly and accurately captioned

____ Craftsmanship is professional (no pencil marks, glue residue, visible tape, etc.)

Total (out of 50 possible points): _____   Due date: _____

Product Research Project Performance Scoring Guide

CRITERIA FOR EVALUATION

Each category is worth 0–10 points

The Written Script

____ Ideas and content—at least 20 relevant facts are embedded in the script

____ Central conflict is relevant, thoughtful, and well developed

____ Conventions (capitalization, punctuation, grammar) are of publishable quality

The Oral Presentation

____ Skit runs 3–5 minutes

____ All parts are perfectly memorized

____ Actors share equally in stage time (no stage hogs, no "ghosts")

____ All actors remain in character throughout the play; all are emotionally engaged; all are costumed appropriately

Total (out of 70 possible points): _____

Product Research Project Commercial Scoring Guide

CRITERIA FOR EVALUATION

Each category is worth 0–10 points

____ Runs 30–45 seconds

____ All product information is true

____ Conventions are of publishable quality

Total (out of 30 possible points): _____

Student Feedback Guidelines

Each student is to fill out feedback forms for the presentations they witness. The focus should be on what you have learned from the presentations, what questions you have based on those presentations, and what suggestions you have for the presenters about how they could make their presentations better. Place your comments on the three-by-five cards you will be given before each presentation.

Sample Project Calendar

Here is one teacher's day-to-day calendar as it actually played out. Jo was quick to point out that it is impossible to plan the speed at which the unit will play out since it depends on the students' abilities to track down useful information, the speed at which their phone calls or emails are returned, and other factors beyond teachers' control. All three classrooms did complete the project during a three-week period.

JO'S CALENDAR:

Sept 25: Introduction of the project—product research project (PRP)

Sept 27: Assigned groups; teacher-chosen

Sept 30: Visit to school library for lessons on how to use Proquest and how to work with Seattle Public Library research materials. Students also learned how to bookmark websites. They presumably have had these skills but needed lots of reminders. The librarian was present for the introduction to the project and is really into it.

Sept 30 also: Students get six questions for their three-person groups; each student has two questions to answer. The questions come from the longer list presented in Chapter 4.

Oct 1–3: Class brainstorms list of possible resources (including the ones suggested here). Class works through group expectations. (This was very difficult for the kids to complete because it was their first group experience of the year.)

Students made job lists: archivist, who keeps track of the papers; director of research, who is willing to line up and make phone calls, among other tasks; designer, who takes charge of how to put it all together. They are all journalists.

Group is charged with compiling a beginning game plan of how they will proceed.

Oct 2: For two days, kids worked on their group jobs and game plans.

Oct 3: Team time in class; then Sweet Honey in the Rock's song, "Are My Hands Clean." Students read and discussed the lyrics and traced the path of the lyrics on a map.

10/8: Class watched *Mickey Mouse Goes to Haiti,* a video that was moderately successful; then the students had workshop time.

10/9: Class watched *Zoned for Slavery* video, which was very effective. The kids took the best notes they've ever taken and were very moved by it.

10/10: The students had workshop time; it took some of them a long time to select their products.

When Jo asked one student why she selected Nike sneakers for her product she replied that it was because she loved Michael Jordan (as if Jordan made the sneakers). This led to an extensive and wonderful discussion about the ways products are advertised and the reasons that students decide what is in and what they will buy.

10/10: "Rage Against the Machine" song and video *Maria,* about a young woman who works in a maquiladora.

10/11: Collected their six questions ... factory information was very difficult to track down.

10/14: Began to plan their posters and skits; two-hour block day.

10/17: Workshop; students also watched a short segment from the video,

When Children Do the Work. This video had to do with the rug makers in Pakistan, and the story of Iqbal Masih, a twelve-year-old worker who escaped and traveled the world, talking about the enslavement of children going on in the rug industry until he was assassinated. Iqbal and working conditions in Pakistan took a few days to discuss. Rugs and soccer balls were the products receiving the most attention.

10/21: Students presented their posters; the weekend before was a very significant time—many groups actually met outside of class and made great strides.

10/25: More posters were presented, and groups rehearsed their skits (they were supposed to present but were not ready).

10/27: Skits were completed.

Follow-up activities are being carried out. There are letter-writing campaigns—to corporations, telling them why they won't be buying their products anymore; to parent groups and school officials saying why the students don't want to use Nike equipment anymore; and to newspapers. Several students participated in the national "Buy Nothing Day," an educational action carried out on the day after Thanksgiving—the busiest shopping day of the year.

5

The Media: Servant of (Too?) Many Masters

The advertiser does not "buy" a news program. He buys an audience.

—Linda Ellerbee

*I*n Carlo Goldoni's classic Commedia "Servant of Two Masters," a clever and ambitious servant named Truffaldino hires himself out to two different men, promising to serve each faithfully. In the ensuing comedy and confusion, Truffaldino juggles and hustles to keep both masters from realizing the true nature of his manipulations, and large quantities of wool are pulled over the eyes of the unsuspecting victims of disinformation. When Truffaldino is forced to confess his crimes in order to be able to marry the woman he loves, his masters are incensed. Each is outraged that Truffaldino wasn't entirely loyal to his (the master's) best interests and that, in fact, his first priority was maximizing his own profit.

Truffaldino's predicament is a bit like the one in which our news media operate. On one hand, the media (at least the individuals working in it) serve an ideal of journalism articulated a century ago by Walter Williams, first dean of the Missouri School of Journalism. "I believe," wrote Williams, "that the public journal is a public trust . . . [and] that acceptance of a lesser service than the public service is betrayal of this trust." Commercial interests, he contended,

88

should play no part in journalism. "I believe . . . that bribery by one's own pocketbook is as much to be avoided as bribery by the pocketbook of another; that individual responsibility may not be escaped by pleading another's instructions or another's dividends" (www.missouri.edu/~jourss/creed.html).

One the other hand, the media operate by corporate laws and values, which have much more to do with the fiduciary duties to their shareholders. In other words, it's all about pocketbooks and dividends.

Price Tags on a Free Press

Virtually all media are privately owned and exist for the purpose of making money, like all other privately run businesses. In the case of television, for example, stations make money by selling advertisements to other companies who are trying to reach those viewing the shows. So, television corporations make money by selling viewers to advertisers. They choose what they will show on their stations (e.g., news, sports, talk shows, sitcoms, cartoons, documentaries) based on what will make them the most money.

The television stations have to assess how much it costs them to make various programs (or to purchase them) and how much advertising money they can sell, which is based on how many viewers they can attract and retain during those shows. Stations charge a certain amount of money to companies that want to advertise their products, charging more for ads run at a time when more people are watching than when fewer people are likely to watch. Media corporations also track who is watching so that they can tell companies this many people watch and they come from a group that has lots of money, so viewers are likely to buy your products. Advertisers sometimes pay more than one million dollars per minute to show their ads during a program like the Super Bowl because so many people watch the game. They will reach many potential buyers of their products, so the expense is worth it to them. If a station identifies the likely audience as young and middle-age men, advertisers run ads tailored to that audience (e.g., shaving cream, cars, beer, business-related things, more cars). They are less likely to pay those dollars to advertise during a program shown at three in the morning.

This process of identifying who views what programs and then linking and targeting viewers with particular advertising is a subset of an analysis process known as *demographics*. Demographers study the characteristics of populations to understand more about who the people are and what they do. Media corporations spend a good deal of time and money learning about their viewers and their habits in order to be able to target them with ads for products the people are likely to want to buy. So while Walter Williams insists that media should serve only the master of the public trust, demographers deconstruct that *public* into myriad special-interest groups, each with its own appetites, interests, agendas, and pocketbooks.

Which Master, or Masters, Do the Media Really Serve?

A fundamental tension, which exists between corporations' responsibilities to make a profit for their stockholders and to keep the citizens aware of what is happening around them (mentioned in the Introduction), is at the heart of the conflict and challenge facing the media and the citizens of this representative democracy. Democracy depends on an informed citizenry, yet we get informed through the media. When this conflicts with the interests of stockholders, corporations have to make decisions about which programs to produce and to show. It is not a simple process.

The lesson activities in this chapter are designed to help students to understand the context in which the media exists and operates; to understand a bit more about the various aspects of those operations; and to help them learn how to function as informed, active citizens through critically observing and using the media.

Students are to consider the ways in which the media appeal to them, and based on those considerations compare, contrast, and critically evaluate the contradictory demands on the media—to make money for its stockholders, to meet its responsibility to inform, to entertain, to facilitate communication. They begin by considering television, then look at print media, including their own textbooks. Students synthesize their learning by creating and applying their insights to their own media.

Analyzing the Media: The Steps

1. Give the students the following brief questionnaire to answer individually:
   - What are your favorite brands of clothing and shoes?
   - What were your favorite brands last year? If you've changed your favorites, why?
   - What are your favorite television shows?
   - What were your favorite shows last year? If you've changed your favorites, why?
   - Which music groups or individual performers are your favorite?
   - Who were they last year? If you've changed your favorites, why?
   - What ordinary household brands of toothpaste, cereal, soda or juice, and fast foods do you and your family buy?
   - How do you and your family decide what brands to buy?

2. Ask students to briefly share responses in small groups of three or four. For the last question, ask the groups to compile a list of the decision-making strategies and factors used by all members in the group.

3. Teacher-led discussion suggestions:
   - Hear about favorite brands. How much agreement or variety is represented?
   - Hear from each group about their compiled lists. How do they decide what to buy?

4. Pose some questions: Do you think you and your family have enough information about the products you buy to make good decisions? What are some kinds of information you might want to know that you don't know yet? For example, what if something you consume on a daily basis isn't really good for you? Would you want to know that? How might you find out? Alternatively, what if something you don't yet consume on a daily basis turns out to be very good for you? Maybe it keeps you healthy so that you live longer and are happier. How would you find out about it? Who is responsible for giving you this kind of information? Should it be on television? In the newspapers? Should your teachers at school make sure you know about it? Is it your parents' responsibility to be informed and tell you?

5. Have the students individually answer some or all of the following questions about *educated* citizenship, either in class or as homework, in preparation for the rest of the unit.
   - Thomas Jefferson said that a democracy could not survive without educated citizens. Do you agree with that statement? Why or why not?
   - What does it mean to be an *educated* citizen? What should citizens in a democracy know so that the democracy will survive?
   - How should people learn about the things an educated citizen should know? Do they have a responsibility to learn these things? When should they learn them?
   - What role should formal education (schools) play in our learning to be educated citizens?
   - What role should the media play in a democracy?
   - What role should families play in helping children to learn about the world?
   - Do you think that most citizens in the United States know what they should know? If not, what kinds of things do you think they don't know?

- What could schools do differently to help citizens learn what they should know?
- What is included in (meant by) the term *the media*?
- What could the media do differently (if you think they could do something differently)?
- Where do you get most of your news and information about the world?
- Do you feel like you are well informed? Why or why not?
- What could you do to get better informed?

6. After students have completed the questionnaire, ask them to share their responses with a partner, and perhaps then with a group of four. This should lead to a whole-class discussion, emphasizing the tension between the need for citizens to know what is going on, the realities of trying to stay informed, and the media corporations' drive for profit.

   Most students will have at least a partial response to what media is (are), and most will include it in their report of how they know what they know about the world. This will serve as a lead-in to learning more about the media, and about how to make best the use of it in service to learning what they need to know as citizens.

7. Ask the students to identify up to five favorite television programs. Have them each pick one or two shows from that list and record the commercials broadcast during that program. The students should then look at the commercials and answer the following questions:

   - Which products are advertised?

   - How are they advertised?

   - Whom do the ads seem to be aimed at (think age group, gender, race or ethnic group, economic level, interests or hobbies, kinds of work)? Whom do advertisers think is watching the show based on the list of commercials students have just compiled?

   - In what ways do you fit the *profile* just compiled for the typical or targeted viewer of that show? In what ways do you not fit the profile?

     Now ask students to watch a show they would normally never watch—a show that would be of no interest to them. Have them record the commercials broadcast during that show and to again analyze those ads and develop a viewer profile for that show based on the same list of questions.

8. Share the results of the preceding question in class after these assignments. You might have students group themselves by shows in common, if possible, to compare and contrast what they have found. The following are some guiding questions for the discussion:

    • What have students noticed about the relationship of shows they watch and the commercials broadcast during those shows?

    • What about the shows they don't watch—whom do they think does watch those shows based on the commercial evidence?

    • What do they conclude from this exercise?

9. Take the investigation a step further by taking a more systematic look at the spectrum of shows offered on television. Have students watch television shows across the viewing spectrum. Here are some sample types of programs: newscasts, cartoons, sports events, prime time sitcoms, teen-oriented shows, programs that seem to be aimed at a specific racial or ethnic group, daytime soaps, morning children's programs, Sunday morning talk shows, *reality* television programs, and so on. Assign groups of two or three students to watch shows and record commercials from some of the shows listed here.

10. Then have them show their commercials to the whole group and ask their classmates to decide who the target audience is based on the commercials they see. Students reveal the particular show's name only after the rest of the group has created a viewer profile based on the commercials.

Television Program Content

Students can take the question of demographics in the media a step further by moving from the advertisements to the programs themselves. This lesson will lead them to look at who they actually see on television, and in what contexts and situations they see them. This exploration is the beginning of a conversation about how we know about ourselves and others, and about whose voices are represented through media, and whose are left out.

Beginning With Students

Have students begin this study by thinking of who they spend their time with, be it family, friends, teachers, bosses, coworkers, members of their church, temple, or mosque, teammates, classmates, and so on. Then, have them identify the people they see on television, in the movies or videos, in books and magazines, or in other media who are purported to be like the people they know. It's a conversation starter aimed at beginning to look at who is included in the conversation about who we are and who is excluded.

Newswatch—Tracking the News

Millions and millions of people in the United States get their news about the rest of the world through television broadcasts. What they know about the world and what they think about what they know depends on what they see on those newscasts. This exercise will help students learn more about what they are seeing on the news.

The beginning exercise for this activity is very simple. Assign students the task of tracking the stories broadcast on various local, national, and, if possible, international newscasts. Have them work in small groups to track the following three categories of data: (1) What stories are broadcast and in what order; (2) Who do they see on the newscasts (including the people broadcasting the news); and (3) What are those people doing? Groups can devise whatever charting system will work best for them, but it's a good idea to model a couple systems they can use, at least as a starting place.

After the groups come back together, you can share the information, comparing and contrasting what they found as a group. You will be able to answer or address questions like these in the discussions:

- What kinds of stories were featured in the news?
- Were there differences between the kinds of stories shown on local and on national newscasts?
- Were there differences between stories featured on U.S. newscasts and those featured on international newscasts (including news from the Canadian broadcasting system or the BBC, which you can find on some cable systems and on the World Wide Web)?
- Who was featured in the stories (gender, race, age, economic level, kind of job or career)?
- What were those persons doing?
- Were there groups who were not represented on the newscast who had an interest in or information about stories that were broadcast? For example, if there were people talking about a possible war, were any of them citizens of the countries involved? People who had relatives in those countries? People who had points of view different from those presented by the administration or experts?
- Who has voice and who does not have voice on our national and local newscasts? Whose points of view are included and whose are excluded or ignored?

Demographics and Regular Programming

It is a short jump to bringing the demographer's eye to the rest of television broadcasting. Students can begin to look at the programs they watch regularly, to assess the ways in which those shows help them to see themselves and the world. They can bring a list of questions to their viewing, and can add to that list as they watch. A starter list of questions might include the following:

- What kind of show is this (comedy, drama, quiz show, teen drama, crime show, reality television, talk show)?
- Brief plot summary: Give a summary of what happens on the show.
- Who are the main characters and what roles do they play (identify by name, gender, ethnic or racial background)?
- Who are the good guys? Who are the bad guys? Who are the heroes? Who are the villains? Who are the actors, who are the victims or passive players? Do these sort out by race, gender, class, or by any other category?
- Who is presented as competent, and who is presented as incompetent, bumbling, or needing help?
- Who solves the problems?

Class members can compare results with what they have found, and work together to understand the picture presented to us through television.

Demographics in the Print Media and Radio

This concept—media demographics, target audiences, and a match between advertising and content—can easily be taken to print media and radio.

Magazines

The activity should begin, as before, with a survey of the magazines the students in your classes actually read. It may be a short list, depending on grade level, with emphasis on teen magazines, sports, specialty *(Road and Track), Mad Magazine* (amazingly still being published), or entertainment. Ask students to select a magazine they really read and to make copies of the large ads within it (if necessary, you can make the copies for them). Have them pose the same set of questions for the television section with minor revisions:

- Which products are being advertised?
- How are they being advertised? What techniques are being used?
- Whom do they seem to be aimed at (age, income, race, interests, work or career choices)? How can you tell?
- How do the students fit (or not) the reader profile they have just compiled?

Have your students bring in their results, again grouping them by similar magazines if that is an option. Conduct a whole-group discussion to share general observations and to connect to what was learned in the television exercise. Now take it a step further by moving beyond magazines normally read by your students.

EXTENDING THE MAGAZINE ACTIVITY

Materials needed—a wide array of magazines of different genres that feature advertisements

Make sure there are women's magazines, such as *Women's Day* or *Working Women* (two different segments of the population); a sports magazine, such as *Sports Illustrated;* a popular culture entry, such as *People;* one focused on teens, such as *Seventeen;* another aimed at seniors, such as *Modern Maturity.* You can also include an example of middle-of-the-road fare like *Time* or *Newsweek;* something a bit left—*The Nation* or *Utne Reader;* something a bit right—*National Review;* some specific niche publications, such as *National Geographic, Scientific American;* financial journals; woodworking or hobbyist journals; publications aimed at particular ethnic or racial populations; and so forth. The wider and more focused the range the better as long as there are ads in the magazines. I also usually include a couple of magazines that are from another era, such as old *Saturday Evening Posts* (from the 1940s), *Life,* or *Look.*

Photocopy at least eight or nine ads from each magazine and clip them together, apart from the magazine; so, for example, all of the ads from the copy of *Time* are clipped together. Place a code number or letter on the front or back page of the pile so that you can quickly identify the magazine from which the ads were pulled. Keep a list of which magazine corresponds to collection number one, number two, and so on. Do this for each magazine so that you have eight or nine piles of advertisements.

Hand out a pile of ads to groups of two or three students. The students' task is to figure out who the advertisers think reads that particular journal or magazine. At what target audiences are the ads aimed? What gender, what age, what income level, what race or ethnic background? What hobbies or interests? What is the communication style? Who are advertisers targeting and how are they trying to appeal to them? The procedure is just what they did for the television assignment and for students' own areas of interest.

Give students fifteen or twenty minutes (more if needed) to look through the ads and develop a reader profile. Then go around the room and hear from each group. After the group has presented, show the magazines from which the ads came. You can debrief the process after the last group presents.

- How close a match was there between the group profiles and the content of the magazine?

- How did the group make their decisions? What factors or features gave them their clues?
- Which magazines were clearest and easiest to identify and which more difficult? Why might that be?

Radio

Radio is another complex media to study, with a fascinating history up through the present day. The Federal Communications Commission Act of 1934, giving over the airways to corporations with an understanding that the airways belonged to the public and should be operated in the public interest, was implemented before television. The act was created in response to the competition and maneuvering (and pressure) for space on the airways exerted by radio stations and the corporations that owned them.

More recent legislation, most notably the updates of the FCC regulations in 1996 and 2003, amended ownership requirements and restrictions such that one company can own more than one radio station in the same market. Companies can in fact own multiple media in the same market (a radio station, a TV station, a newspaper, for example). Clear Channel is a modern example of a corporation that owns many radio stations across the country, often several in one city. The result is that more and more programming is being created by the same studios, and more and more shows are broadcast nationally. There is speculation that this is narrowing the choices available to listeners across the country and eliminating the local aspect of radio.

RADIO ACTIVITY

Begin by asking students what they listen to during a typical day or week. Have them chart their listening habits, by station and hour for the week. As a class, compare the lists to see what range of stations students listen to as a group. This can be done anonymously, or by having students turn their logs in to you so that you can simply read the stations and time. Thus, someone who listens to an unpopular station need not admit to it in front of his or her peers; life's tough enough.

Have students track the songs they hear on music stations for a certain amount of time; this can be done as a tag team, with someone taking the first hour, someone else the next, and so on. Other students can track the topics covered on various talk radio shows. Another group can monitor what is available on student stations, low-power community radio stations (some of which operate illegally—pirate stations), and NPR affiliates. The reports can lead to a wonderful discussion about what it is possible to hear or not hear, and can offer some possibilities for further research.

Students could also conduct an analysis of the kinds of songs that are popular for this year, and work backward for the past ten years; this lesson was presented in some detail in *Living History in the Classroom* (Selwyn 1993). They would pay attention to who is singing or playing the music, what the style of music is, and what the music is about in terms of both topic and point of view. They might investigate those songs on top of the charts in various categories to see if there is any consistency or divergence from genre to genre. They might also research the kinds of music that did not receive airplay during those years. African American performers, for example, were kept off all but one or two stations per market for many decades in the early years of radio. Are there modern-day equivalents to that experience?

Commercialism in the Schools

There is a growing movement across the country against the increased commercialism in public schools. There is concern about the junk food that is being sold to students in vending machines and, in some locations, by in-school fast-food outlets. The coalition of groups opposing this commercialism is concerned with it as both a health issue—the astounding and alarming increase in obesity and the onset of adult diabetes in twelve- to fourteen-year-old students—and an invasion of students' privacy. There is concern that public schools, which serve as legal guardians (in loco parentis) for the students who attend, have a responsibility to shield them from corporations who would prey on them.

Advertising and commercialism takes many forms in schools, from vending machines dispensing soda and other drinks from a particular company (which often has an exclusive contract with a school district), to fast-food outlets, to displays featuring products. Students are often routed to particular publishers' book clubs that also offer posters displaying their logo to be placed at the school.

The task of selling candy or other products to raise money for particular events is often assigned to students. This issue clearly intersects with the larger issue of school funding, because students are selling commercial products to fund activities not covered in school district budgets.

Textbooks and the products of textbook and other publishing companies include references to and advertising for their other products. Walls are often adorned with *free* posters sporting corporate logos, and teachers carry or use supplies given to them at conferences by educational houses that are only too happy to support them with free gifts, much the same as drug companies that provide doctors with samples, prescription pads, mugs, and pens.

Let us not forget Channel One. This privately owned media channel is mandated viewing in many schools around the country. Schools agree to require their students to watch the programming, including commercials, on a daily basis. In exchange, the owners of Channel One provide VCRs and other equipment to the schools; students are being "sold" to the channel's advertisers in exchange for equipment that schools without extensive media budgets cannot otherwise afford.

COMMERCIALISM ACTIVITIES

Have students conduct a walkthrough of their school, identifying the ways in which advertising and commercialism are present. This can be done easily from tee shirts, posters, clothes labels; to vending machines, book covers or folders, or other school-related supplies featuring a brand name or label; to recruitment posters for the armed forces, particular companies, or colleges and universities. Then, students can identify the products advertised and the ways in which these ads are designed.

It would be a wonderful follow-up step to perform the same analysis of these ads as they are conducted with respect to television and print advertising detailed earlier in the chapter. How are advertisers targeting them, and how are they viewed as a target audience by advertisers?

There is a step-by-step guide to doing commercialism walkthroughs on the Citizens' Campaign for Commercial Free Schools website *(www.scn.org/cccs)*. The site offers suggestions of things to look for and questions to ask teachers, students, administrators, and parents involved with the school community. The guidelines suggest that all of the groups should be interviewed in order to fully understand the extent that commercialism is present in the school community.

Finally, students can decide what steps, if any, to take in response to what they have found. They can do a presentation to the school about the impact that commercialism is having on their lives at school. They could do anticommercialism advertising in the spirit of the Adbusters group from British Columbia, Canada, which uses the techniques of advertising to counter commercialism (see *www.adbusters.org*). Students could design a presentation for the local school board in terms of their concerns regarding commercialization of the schools. They could approach the PTSA or other parent and community groups to register their concerns and to help enlist adult support.

Ownership of the Media

Who decides what is in the textbook, on the radio, on television programs or the news, in newspapers and journals, or in the movies? How is it that a few individuals get to decide what news and entertainment we (the public) get to see and hear? How does the ability of those few individuals to determine what we (the public) see and hear potentially contradict the needs of a democratic country to have informed citizens? What does it mean that there are fewer and fewer corporations and/or individuals who own the media on which we depend?

To begin a discussion, ask your students the following kinds of questions: What kinds of media play a role in your life? What do you watch, listen to, read, or somehow come in contact with as an individual and as a member of your community? More specifically, you can ask: which radio station do you listen to? What are your favorite shows and/or songs? Which television stations do you watch? What are four or five of your favorite movies of the past year or two? What are your favorite books of the past year? Which textbooks do you use at school? Which newspapers, magazines, or journals do you read?

Have students answer the following questions about at least one radio station, one television station, and one magazine or newspaper or journal:

- Who owns the television station(s) you watch most? Who owns the station locally and who owns it nationally? What else do they own?
- What kind of music do you listen to?
- Which radio stations do you listen to most often? Who owns those stations? What else do they own?
- Who decides the play list, guest list, or content of the programming you listen to or watch?
- How often do you feel that your views are accurately represented in the media you use? This can be specific—someone asks you what you think—or general—they don't ask me, but they are saying what I would say.
- How often do you feel well served by the media in terms of helping you know what you need to in order to be an informed citizen?

Textbook Analysis

Textbooks are media too. Traditionally, they have been geared to sell to school districts in California and Texas primarily because those states offer huge markets. As a result, the texts are written in a way that will not offend those markets and that will appeal to them. What does this mean for students? What choices might textbook publishers make, keeping this economic reality in mind? What will they choose to include, to exclude? How will they present that material?

Students don't always think about their textbooks as media, and it's doubtful that they would think about them as having a point of view or a bias. It is a very useful exercise to help them learn more about textbook analysis, to help them to understand what they are and are not getting. The following are some sample or guiding questions to begin a textbook analysis:

- How is the book organized?
- What is the overall structure for this look at the topic?
- Is it organized by geographical region, or simply year by year, or via some kind of theme?
- Is there any connection or relationship between one part of the book and another? Is history seen as a continuous process or as a series of discreet episodes virtually disconnected from each other?
- What are the chapter titles in the book? Do they reflect any particular point of view? For example, if a chapter in U.S. History is entitled something like "The Age of Exploration," it is clear that the writers are presenting a European American point of view. Whose story is being told, and by whom?
- What do you see in the photographs and drawings that are used? Who is featured and what are they doing? Does there seem to be diversity and balance? Are representatives of the full population presented in a respectful and representative way?
- What are the main points of each chapter? Are items presented in context or simply in succession, year by year? Whose history is being presented?
- Who is speaking for the various points of view? Are there points of view either not represented, or defined by others (a European or European American defining a Native American point of view, for example)? Is there an inappropriate grouping of points of view (the Native American point of view, for example, as if there were only one view shared by all Native American people)?
- Are certain populations reduced to the sidebars of the book, with feature stories on some individuals as if they are outside the mainstream of history? Are they portrayed as exotic, or quaint, or primitive? Do Native Americans, for example, appear only in stereotypical dress and only as some tribes might have been hundreds of years ago on the plains?
- Are women portrayed as more than helpers to men? Are they portrayed at all?
- Is there room for controversy or disagreement about historical events and what they mean?
- Is there any discussion about the different ways in which various historians

and populations interpret what has happened in history and what it means?

- How does a historian's account (Howard Zinn's *People's History of the United States* is a good source to contrast with other U.S. history textbooks) of a particular event or time compare with a textbook's account of the same event or time period? How are they similar, how are they different? How do you understand or explain or deal with the differences?

- What kinds of learning and activities are students expected to do with relation to this book? Are they expected to answer fact-based questions at the end of chapters? Are there invitations to engage in the research about complex, complicated questions leading to a more complete understanding of why things are the way they are?

- What resources and references have authors cited? Do they seem to represent a spectrum of recent knowledge, thought, and scholarship in the field? Are there resources from within various communities that present their own points of view about history?

- How do the authors of the textbook support the history and interpretations they present? Do they make a case for their conclusions or points of view or do they simply present what they offer as indisputable fact, with no evidence or explanation?

Literature

This same principle can be applied to the literature that students read in their classrooms and on their own. Helping students to evaluate the fiction they read for the same elements concerning point of view and bias can help them understand what they are reading as a historian might.

The Council on Interracial Books for Children, Professor James Banks of the University of Washington, the teachers and writers at Rethinking Schools, and many other groups and individuals have offered outlines or approaches for book analysis as well. Formulate an outline to share with your students, or encourage them to develop their own strategies for evaluating the materials they read.

The Council on Interracial Books for Children suggests paying attention to the following categories:

- *Illustrations:* Check illustrations for stereotypes in terms of how people are portrayed, for tokenism (slightly darker versions of whites), for stereotypes in what the people portrayed are doing.

- *Story line:* What is the basic story line of the book? What is the standard for success and how do the major characters attain it? Do characters of color depend on help from white characters? Are female characters less active or skilled than male characters? Are African American characters succeeding more because of physical skills than academic ones?

- *Lifestyles:* How are the daily lives of the characters portrayed? Are characters of color portrayed as living in a manner somehow inferior to the white, middle-class norm? Are people of color living exclusively in ghettoes or slums? Is there really information about the ways in which people live or are there gross generalizations? Are people of color presented as quaint or exotic rather than as real people living their lives?

- *Relationships among people:* Who possesses the power in the story? Who exercises leadership and intelligence and ingenuity? How do families function? How do various members within families deal with each other? How do characters communicate with characters across racial, gender, and other lines? Is there equality?

- *Reader's self-image:* How might children respond to the story? How will it make them feel about themselves and their place in the world?

- *Consider the author's or illustrator's perspective and background:* Who are they and how are they qualified to write the story (or to draw the illustrations)? Where have they lived? What resources have they consulted or referred to? What do they know in order to write what they have written? Can their work (can they) be trusted to fairly represent the world in ways that are not biased, intentionally or unintentionally, or inaccurate?

- *Vocabulary:* Are *loaded* words—ones that carry a stereotypical overtone about a particular race, ethnicity, gender, or class of people—used in the story?

- *Age of the story:* Stories often represent the attitudes, knowledge, and prejudices of their time and place. Books written before the early 1970s tend to reflect values that contained prejudice and sexist attitudes. It would be especially important to examine stories written before this time to make sure that the messages they contain are ones you want your students to see. It is also important to help students recognize and understand the bias and prejudice contained in some literature.

The Power of the Images in the Arts

This same set of questions can be applied to children's literature be it fiction or nonfiction. It is important to note that while fiction is not written to be as rigorous as a social studies text, it does serve the function of helping us to know more about particular times, places, and people. The fact that literature generally presents more fully developed characters in settings that are more artfully described means that the images and scenes are vivid for readers, and that they may stay with them as lasting images of a time and a place.

A Tale of Two Cities is more likely to help form people's impressions of France in the late eighteenth century than a textbook paragraph about that time. Many people came to *know* about Japan through the novel and miniseries *Shogun,* which was only partially accurate. The images from the television series and from the very detailed descriptions of the novel are likely more powerful than the one-sentence or one-page summary of Japanese history in relation to the Europeans in your textbook.

One of the consequences of that is the tremendous amount of misinformation about what the world is, or was, like when presented through inaccurate or incomplete histories in literature. This makes it very important to help students bring their critical thinking and viewing skills to the literature that they read and the movies that they see.

Movies

The images and story lines of movies are so intense and so carefully crafted that they are very convincing in what they present, even when some of the information is incorrect. Students come to school with enormous amounts of misinformation based on movies they have watched; most moviemakers have little interest or concern about historical accuracy. Usually, movies feature a hero who fights a simplified villain and triumphs over adversity, or fails with glory and honor and a lasting legacy. This may or may not resemble what actually happened, and may or may not fairly represent the people who were involved in the incidents portrayed.

The images are compelling, the story lines clear and evocative, and the movies are both fictional and memorable. The consequences for us as social studies teachers is that we have to undo the mis-education our students have suffered before; we need to help them learn a more accurate and useful approach to the study of history.

Stereotypes and Socialization

The discussions and lessons about stereotyping and socialization throughout this chapter also apply to the movies. Images and models of race, class, and gender throughout the history of moviemaking have shaped millions of viewers' attitudes around the world. Big-budget films—from the virulently racist (and celebrated) *Birth of a Nation,* created at the dawn of cinema; to the epic (and racist) "mis-histories" of *Gone with the Wind, Lawrence of Arabia,* and *The Alamo;* to the escapist adventures of *Indiana Jones, James Bond, Spiderman,* and the *Star Wars* series; and on to the current blockbusters playing in your area's multiplexes—carry information (or *mis*information) about the peoples and places of this world and beyond. Movies are not value-neutral, and the fact that they are created with entertainment in mind does little to minimize their message or impact. We can help students bring the same critical rigor that they bring to the television they watch, the magazines and books they read, and the media they rely on for news to the movies they view.

Movies reflect the values of a certain segment of the population because film studios finance and produce movies they think will make money—that is, people will pay to see them. Movie producers focus on satisfying the public's desire for entertainment, so historical accuracy is the last thing on their minds, as well as those of most moviegoers. The choices made, from what stories get made into movies, to the kinds of movies that are made from those stories, to who acts in them, to how they are promoted are all business decisions.

As in virtually all other aspects of the media, the golden rule applies: the one who has the gold rules. The decision makers at large studios decide what images we will see, what history we will revisit, and what stories we will never see told on the big screen. Those decisions and the studios' products may or may not reflect *reality*, but they will have an immense impact on what people know, or think they know, about the world.

A Movie Activity

Have students track the most popular movies of the past twenty-five years, year by year. This should work out to approximately one year per student; you can go back in time one year for each additional student. Some of these movies are likely to be R rated ones, so students can either consult film guides, newspaper reviews, or journals that summarize plots and identify characters and actors because they can't legally watch the movies. Have students identify their favorite movies for the past five years, and carry out the exercise by asking them to answer the following questions:

- What is the title of the movie?
- What kind of movie is it (action, comedy, spy vs. spy, love story, sports-oriented)?
- Give a summary of the plot in a paragraph.
- Who are the main characters? Include their race and gender.
- What are they like? How do they behave? Are they realistic characters, or stereotypes?
- How do they interact with each other?
- What values, assumptions, and beliefs seem to underlie the movie?
- Is the movie based on actual historical situations in any way? If so, how does the movie treat the topic? How does that match historical information about the event or situation?

- Which studio made the movie? Who owns the studio? What else do they own?
- Are connections made between the movie and other products owned by the parent company (the company that owns the movie studio and other companies)? For example, are action figures from the movie being sold or offered at fast-food outlets?

The Media and the Public's Need to Know

What most people in the United States know about the world and the events that happen in it comes from the *mainstream* media. Readers of local papers, such as the *Los Angeles Times, The Boston Globe, The Chicago Tribune, The Denver Post,* or *The Dallas Morning News,* or even national papers such as *The New York Times* or *USA Today,* assume that they are getting accurate, relatively complete, and unbiased information they can rely on. In the past, these assumptions have often proved to be false, and it would seem to be worthwhile to question them again.

The following lesson activities will encourage students to investigate the role that point of view plays in determining the information they have access to, and the reliability of that information. If you have done any of the activities described in Chapters 2 and 3 (e.g., The History of the Class, or collages), this is an opportunity to make connections; refer back to those activities and review them to reinforce the lesson at hand.

A range of newspaper and journal articles about an event or issue that is particularly relevant, important, and of interest as a current event will be needed. Bookstores, newsstands, and libraries in most cities offer a range of newspapers and journals. Many of the same publications, plus hundreds of others, are available on the Internet. Select articles from across the political and economic spectrum.

> Sources from the progressive end of the spectrum include Znet *(www.zmag.org),* common dreams *(www.commondreams.org),* The Progressive *(www.theprogressive.org),* the independent media center *(www.indymedia.org), The Nation (www.thenation.org),* alternet *(www.alternet.org),* and the Rouge Forum *(www.pipeline.com/~rgibson/rouge_forum/).*

> More moderate sources include *Time* and *Newsweek* magazines, *The New York Times (www.nytimes.com),* the news pages of *the Wall Street Journal (www.wsj.com)* (their editorials are very conservative), the *Christian Science Monitor (www.csmonitor.com),* and many daily papers across the country.

The more conservative sources include the *National Review* (*www.nationalreview.com*), the *American Spectator* (*www.spectator.org*), *Forbes* (*www.forbes.com*), and *The Weekly Standard* (*www.weeklystandard.com*).

You will also want to include news sources from other countries. There are a couple of websites that make this task easier than it might seem for students to collect news from around the world; three of them are *www.dailyearth.com, http://newslink.org,* and world press review (*www.worldpress.org*).

The Economist comes at its material from a relatively conservative, economics-centered viewpoint *(www.economist.com). The International Herald Tribune (www.iht.com)* combines resources of *The New York Times* and *The Washington Post* and it has an overseas eye for a slightly different perspective.

Neighborhood journals and papers from various local communities may or may not have a perspective to share on national and international events but are good sources to have available.

This is, of course, a partial list—a starter set of resources until you can find your own favorites.

Contrasting Media Accounts: The Steps

Make sure that the groups are researching articles that span the spectrum of political orientations. You can provide articles from the sources just listed (or your own sources), or you can assign students the task of finding their own articles. If you make this latter choice, you must monitor them to ensure that you still have the full spectrum of viewpoints represented in the articles read. Students can read the articles in class (if you have them on hand and already copied), or you can assign the reading as homework. Groups will need class time to share their ideas about the articles and to decide what to communicate to their classmates.

1. Ask students what they know about a particular event or issue that is significant and of the moment. You'll want to have students share what they know of the historical context of the situation, the factors that are present in this current situation, and how this current situation can be understood in its historical context.

2. After that, ask them how they know what they know. Where do they get their information? What are their sources? Why do they trust these sources?

3. Next, assign groups of three students to read an article about the event or issue from a particular point of view, and to write a summary of the reporter's main points. This should work out to nine or ten groups in a typical classroom, which will offer the class the opportunity to experience a wide range of views about the event. Students should first present the article without their own views and questions: What does the writer say in his or her article? On what do they base their opinions or presentation? The students can then include their own questions and reactions to the article and share whether the journalist is confirming what they already know or believe, or challenging their knowledge.

4. Come back together as a whole class and chart the major points made by each article. On which points does there seem to be agreement? On which points are there major disagreements? Is there a presentation of the context or history of the situation in these articles, and is there agreement about that? What seems most unclear from the collection of articles? What would be good areas for further research? Where would you go to research these points?

5. End with a closure discussion. The following are some possible questions: How typical or atypical is this range of points of view when it comes to what we hear or read as news? Is the range of viewpoints and coverage you found specific to the particular topic you researched, or is it more the *rule*? Why is it that many of the ideas and points of view offered in these articles are not ones you've heard before? Does this mean they are wrong? How do we evaluate information for reliability and accuracy? How can we keep informed on world issues when we are offered such a narrow range of information by the mainstream media? What strategies can people develop for staying informed about what is happening in the world? Why is that important? Is it important?

A Cautionary Note: Adjusting to Reading Levels

I never assume that an ability to read is the same thing as an ability to understand and to discuss complex issues; I have had wonderful and insightful discussions with students who could not easily read the text. If some or most of your students are likely to struggle with reading the articles you have gathered, you must consider some strategies for helping them to gain access to the articles so that you can have informed discussions. The following are several options:

• Read all the articles out loud to the entire class and deal with the range of points of view together as a whole group. It would take time to read the eight or nine articles, but students would hear them all and would be able to participate in the discussion.

- Read them and then send the groups out to reread and prepare summaries of each article as described before. They would be supported by the oral reading you have done, which might be enough to enable students to present an accurate and useful summary of the article for a class discussion.

- Choose three or four articles to read aloud rather than all eight or nine. Select articles that reflect the range of attitudes and viewpoints on the issue in question, so that you can discuss the role that point of view plays in what we get to read, hear, and know about an issue or situation. Obviously, choosing three or four articles to read takes less class time than reading all of them.

- Rewrite three or four articles such that you keep the points of view and arguments of the authors while recasting the text at an appropriate reading level for your students.

- Ask volunteers to help you by reading each article onto a tape so that class members can listen to the articles as they read them.

- Encourage students to work together to help each other make sense of the text as best they can, then have them work with the ideas as a group.

Extensions
Here are several possible extensions for this assignment:

- Carry out the research activities identified by the group during the discussion. After reading the collection of articles, find out more about unclear or disputed aspects of your chosen topic.

- Have students write an article based on their new understanding of the situation, either in the style of one of the articles they've read or in their own voice.

- Have students identify voices they have not heard from, those who might have insight and information about the situation. For example, Sarah MacFarlane's class looked more closely at the then-proposed U.S. attack on Iraq (see next section). She might ask her students to focus on locating members of the Seattle Iraqi community, who have not been included in media coverage, to get their perspective on what is happening. They might also locate articles from Israel, Arab neighbors in the Middle East, or articles from interested parties such as France or Russia—both countries are very interested in Iraq's oil reserves. Who else might add to an understanding of the situation?

- Have students carry out a campaign to share what they have learned with others via letters to the editor, communications with elected officials, an information session with other classes, a presentation to their local PTSA, a relevant community group, or at a community rally.

- Carry out the same activity on other topics, identifying the ways in which various journals or newspapers cover particular items.

- Do the same activity with different media, especially television and radio. What views are offered, which withheld? Who determines what is seen? Who is represented, and who is missing? What options are there for experiencing a wider range of views?

When It's Not in Your Schedule, But It Is in the News

Sarah Heller MacFarlane, a high school teacher in the Shoreline School District near Seattle, worked with the idea of *multiple sources* of information as a way of helping her students to more fully understand what was at the time (December 2002) happening and threatening to happen in Iraq. She felt only able to devote a week to the lesson, given the amount of material she had already mapped out for her first semester geography classes, but the impending U.S. invasion of Iraq was too large of a current event to ignore.

Sarah began by asking her students to respond to the educated citizen questionnaire included in the *Analyzing the Media* section at the beginning of this chapter. She wanted her students to reflect on what they thought they should know about the world, what they felt they actually knew about the world, how they knew it, and then to think about what they did not know. The student responses led to a very promising discussion of the role that media played in their lives.

The students had a class discussion about what they knew or did not know about the situation in Iraq, focusing on both what they knew (factual information) and what kinds of information they knew. They also focused on what kinds of information they knew little or nothing about, and discussed why that might be so.

Then Sarah assigned students the task of reading at least three articles dealing with the situation in Iraq from across the *political* spectrum. Since two of the overarching goals for this class throughout the semester were to focus on learning to classify information and to develop critical-thinking skills, this assignment fit right into that framework.

Students' first task was to identify three facts and three opinions for each article. They were then to classify the articles as either arguments supporting an invasion of Iraq, or arguments opposing it, anchoring their classifications with information in the articles' text.

The next task was to identify which vocabulary terms were used in each article and how they were used. The term *terrorism*, for example, was not used in the same way in every article the students read, nor did it always refer to the same people. The students identified what they felt to be *loaded* terms across the spectrum and noted the different ways they appeared in the various stories they read.

Finally, the students conducted a debate about the situation; should an attack against Iraq be launched? Sarah did not assign sides to the debate until ten minutes before it began, so students had to be ready and able to argue from either view point. She allowed the students to choose a side for the last ten minutes of the debate so that they could switch, if they wanted to, for those last few minutes.

She had the students write a reflective summary about the debate, noting which arguments were strongest and most persuasive. They could also talk about whether they had changed their minds as the debate continued, or whether their views had strengthened.

Like Sarah MacFarlane, Wendy Ewbank, a seventh-grade social studies teacher at the Seattle Girls School, had neither U.S.–Iraqi relations nor current events on her December 2002 schedule. Nonetheless, she felt the UN ultimatum Iraq was under to deliver a report about its "weapons of mass destruction" program by December 8, 2002, with potentially catastrophic consequences if it failed to do so, was too important and immediate a situation to ignore. She also decided that the lessons learned in an assignment concerning the media's points of view, and its impact on what we know about the world, would serve her and her students well throughout their studies for the rest of the year.

Wendy constructed a three-day assignment using a lesson plan design from a social studies journal as the underlying structure. That lesson plan, presented under the title "Crisis with Iraq: Policy Options" in the November/December edition of *Social Education* (2002, 410–411), gives students three possible U.S. policy options for dealing with Iraq, and then directs them to develop a fourth policy option of their own. The lesson includes the three policy options and offers a brief summary of the goals, line of reasoning, underlying beliefs, and criticism of each. The students were to offer their own intended goals, underlying assumptions, plans, and possible criticism for the policy option they developed.

The first step in the process was for all of the students to read an article from *Time for Kids*—"The Struggle Over Iraq," by Ritu Upadhyay (11 October 2002). The article's point of view is very much in line with the mainstream, middle-of-the-road coverage offered in daily papers, and gives students general, basic information about the situation in Iraq. After they read the article, Wendy divided the class in half and gave each half different articles to read.

Half read a pair of articles from the U.S. media on the Iraq situation. The first article was "Ten Reasons Why Many Gulf War Veterans Oppose Re-Invading Iraq," which was written by an anonymous Gulf War veteran; it was posted on the Common Dreams website (*www.commondreams.org*, 13 September 2002). The article presents the author's personal view about the possibility of war based on his experiences during the Gulf War in 1991. The second article, "In Iraqi War Scenario, Oil Is Key Issue: US Drillers Eye Huge Petroleum Pool," was written by Dan Morgan and David Ottaway (*Washington Post,* 15 September 2002). The article focuses on the role that oil is playing in the decision about whether to go to war in Iraq. These articles were very different from each other and from the article the students had read in *Time for Kids.* The other half of the class read a series of articles from Arabic newspapers that Wendy had pulled together; they expressed a range of views from the Arabic community, and were taken from the world press review website (*www.worldpress.org*).

The students were directed to highlight or identify information in their articles that was new to them, or contained something significant that they had not heard or read before. They then worked in groups of four (two students from each half of the room) to process what they had learned from their articles and to attempt to make sense of the information and points of view.

After they were done processing the articles, those same groups of four students worked together to carry out the assignment outlined in the *Social Education* article. Their task was to formulate a fourth policy option in addition to the three included in the article for the U.S. to consider in its dealings with Iraq. They were to provide their goals for the situation, their underlying assumptions, their suggested policy option, possible concerns about that policy option, and options for meeting the goals. They were to create posters communicating this information to their classmates. The students continued to work in their groups to prepare the posters. Here are two summaries of their work.

> *Goals:* Work with the United Nations to stop Saddam from threatening others; arrange for the UN weapon inspectors to go to Iraq; reduce our visibility in the region to avoid terrorist attacks against the U.S.; improve our relationships with Iraq's neighbors by increasing financial aid.

The Plan:
- We'll plan with the UN so that if Saddam threatens anyone we can arrest him and bring him to court.
- We'll arrange so that the UN can have weapon inspectors go search Iraq.
- Not be first in line and seem so controlling, to reduce visibility.
- To improve our relationships with Iraq's neighbors by improving financial aid, and giving more supplies, food money, etc.

—Jamie and Kendal

Goals: To take Saddam out of power; to bolster the Iraqi economy, and make it a democracy; to create world security; to remove all weapons of mass destruction.

Plan: First, we must find proof to show that Saddam does have weapons of mass destruction. Haul Saddam off to a crimes tribunal for violating Gulf War cease fire. Have Iraqi people reelect their own president. Take off U.S. sanctions on Iraq and build their economy over.

Note at bottom: No Iraq War! Attack Iraq? No!!!

—Piper, Anne, Dee T., Kim, Bianca

Wendy noted that this quick study of the situation in Iraq would likely form the basis for additional study after the holiday break.

Once the war in Iraq started, the need for critical analysis and multiple sources advocated in this lesson plan became even more evident. Fox News, CNN, and other mainstream sources focused on the technological expertise of the U.S. military, featuring smart bombs and precision bombing, the speed of the ground advance across the Iraqi desert, and the clarity and precision of the mission (oust Saddam in order to liberate the Iraqi people).

Progressive news outlets such as Common Dreams or the Progressive website emphasized the horrors of war, the thousands of innocent Iraqi civilians being killed, wounded, and traumatized, and the lust for oil and empire driving this illegal U.S. invasion of a sovereign nation.

The world press offered a wider range of views and emphases, from the illegality of the U.S. invasion to the concerted coalition effort to liberate the people of Iraq, to calls rallying Arabs throughout the region to stand up to Bush and his imperialist armies.

It is clear that no one source has full claim on the truth of the conflict, or of the underlying reasons for it. The historian and student who tries to research the situation fully must listen to all of the relevant voices and points of view as critically and patiently as possible, to move past the hysteria and emotion of the moment in order to attain understanding.

It is an approach that flies in the face of the media push for instant news ("See first live pictures tonight at 11:00!") and sound bites that sum up complicated situations and stories in ten seconds or less. All the more reason to have students practice this approach and learn to apply it to the events of their world.

Learning It by Doing It

There is no better way for students to learn about the media than by making their own. Technology has evolved to the point that creating newspapers, for example, is a very simple activity for anyone with a basic word processing program. I have seen them done often at the elementary school level, and done relatively professionally at the high school grades. It can also be done without computer technology; cut and paste still works, and the lessons learned are still of high value. Video filming and editing are both increasingly within reach, too, as camera prices plunge and user-friendly computer editing programs become standard software on newer models. As with print media, though, you can get good results with some basic techniques and equipment. These next lesson activities look at how students can create their own media, taking on the roles of reporters and producers of news.

Clarifying Objectives: A Lesson, a Unit, an Entire Course?

The most important challenges facing teachers working with multistep projects, such as creating a newspaper or newscast, is being clear about objectives. Creating a newspaper requires skills in conducting research, in learning about history or particular content areas, in working in groups and teams, in writing, in editing, and in making judgments about the overall newspaper format, design, and layout. Creating a newscast involves many of the same skills, with added requirements such as thinking visually, distilling complex information into manageable sound bites, and learning poise and presence in front of a camera.

It is too much for students to learn all at once. They must have the time and support they need in each area to be able to learn productively, and then have the opportunity to pull it all together in a meaningful way. Breaking a project into manageable chunks is often an approach that produces good results for everyone. You might want to choose to emphasize one aspect of the process if students have not had much experience with carrying out the full range of skills necessary. You might, for example, study the parts of a newspaper at one time during the year, followed by the ways in which reporters do research for articles they are writing. A separate unit could concentrate on various types of writing (factual, editorial, interview, opinion). Then you can carry out another newspaper project later in the year to allow them to bring together the full spectrum of what they have learned.

For a newscast project, you might precede it by practicing on-camera presence in an unrelated language arts/communication unit and familiarizing students with various formats of television news content coverage by support-ing learning in other units of study. This could include viewing videodocu-mentaries, such as *The Civil War*, or *The Twentieth Century;* seeing excerpts from interview shows, such as *Charlie Rose* and *Larry King Live;* and watching excerpts from television magazine-format shows such as *20/20* and *60 Minutes.* Later, you might analyze the elements of a newscast and compare and contrast this format with others you've seen earlier in the year.

Meanwhile, your language arts curriculum could include a focus on the kinds of writing skills needed to produce effective television messages. As with a newspaper project, a newscast could then be the culminating unit that enables students to synthesize a full semester or a year of learning a variety of skills.

Living History in the Classroom (Selwyn 1993) describes the process for creating either a newspaper or a newscast. It is a comprehensive and integra-tive project that brings together a variety of skills including research, working as a member of a group, writing (expository, persuasive, narrative, technical), social studies (history, geography, civics, economics), and various aspects of media literacy. A project can be carried out in a week or developed to pull together a full quarter's work. The elements of the process are similar at all grade levels; the differences lie in the content and in the skills and experiences that students bring to the project.

A Basic Model for Creating Newspapers

I will present a brief overview of how the model might work and then offer examples of how it has played out in a couple of classrooms. We begin our work by launching inquiries in two different directions. One line of inquiry is concerned with learning about newspapers and how they are put together. The second line of inquiry is concerned with the actual content, which could reflect schools, businesses, current events, historical issues (the Civil War, the American Revolution, the Russian Revolution), or other themes, that will appear in the paper.

1. Learning about the process of creating newspapers includes learning about the different forms of material that appear in newspapers

(reporting, opinion columns, editorials, editorial cartoons, public service notices, community awareness notices, advertisements, classified listings, science or technical information, and so on). We also need to identify the various sections of the paper, including national news, local news, sports, arts and entertainment, classified, science and technology, editorial and opinion, comics, obituaries, and whatever else we notice. I help students to understand what goes into each section of the paper and to realize that what they see each day is a result of conscious decisions made by an editorial team, which decides what to include and what to leave out.

2. Students practice identifying facts and opinions. Facts are verifiable by someone who is not the speaker (or writer) as either true or false; opinions cannot be verified by anyone else. "It is raining today" is a fact—maybe true, maybe false, but easily verified by someone else. "Weapons containing depleted Uranium should never have been used in Iraq, in Kosovo, or anywhere else," is an opinion that cannot be definitively proved true or false; it depends on the point of view and judgment of the speaker. Saying an opinion over and over does not make it a fact, although this is an approach taken by many politicians, journalists, and students. It is useful for students to learn this important distinction.

3. We also work at understanding the five Ws and one H of basic reporting (who, what, when, where, why, and how), and the challenge of taking lots of information and presenting it clearly in a brief column. Students also need to learn to write about complex situations and issues in ways that make them understandable to an average reader. They should read various columnists in order to understand how to tell a story that has more than one point of view.

4. Learning about content involves having students research the various content items that will form the basis for the paper. You, as editor in chief, can make a basic list of what you want covered, guided by what you want the students to know about at the end of your unit of study. Include student input as much as is appropriate for your grade level and particular students, and encourage everyone to research relevant items of particular interest to them.

5. Assign the news stories to teams of two, with some attention to who researches which story based on your assessment of student skills and interests. Give students a clear timeline for the various stages of the project: have your research plan after two days, research notes after

a week, story's first draft after eight days, final story in two weeks—
or whatever schedule fits your students and topic. As editor, you
should check in with each group to monitor progress, offer guidance
and research suggestions as needed, and serve as cheerleader and
taskmaster. Teams might be placed in charge of creating opinion
columns or editorials, and it would serve you well to have editorials
presenting differing points of view on various topics or issues.

6. One team of students might be in charge of locating appropriate
   graphics (photographs, drawings, charts, maps, etc.). Others might be
   more involved in layout and physical operations. Given today's
   powerful computers, a simple word processing program allows you to
   place writing in two or three columns at the touch of a button and
   then layout becomes a simple matter of moving work around the
   page until it fits together nicely. Students might need to adjust the font
   size (slightly smaller or larger) to help fit the material on the page, and
   they can always edit a bit for length if needed.

NEWSPAPER EXAMPLES FROM PRODUCT RESEARCH PROJECTS

Students in the seventh-grade classes at the Summit K–12 School in Seattle
wrote various kinds of newspaper articles based on the research they conducted
on the manufacturing of ordinary objects (see Chapter 4). Some wrote as
reporters on the scene in the countries where the factories are; some wrote
letters to the editor, presumably in response to an article about slave labor
(really based on their own research); and others chose to write editorials aimed
at audiences in the United States, where the products were purchased.

Nicholas, writing a straight news story for the *Summit Times,* reported: "Twenty-
four-year-old Marashalene Ramaliehe was stabbed while protesting the poor
working conditions in a Gap sweatshop in Lesotho. She was stabbed in the
neck with sharp scissors by the factory director." The attack was caught on
videotape, which can be seen at *www.behindthelabel.com.*

Kayce concluded her Letter to the Editor with a plea to increase coverage of labor
issues. "Please, I am asking you to post more information in your newspaper
about sweatshops and tell everyone how they are being treated, so people can
realize how good they have it and try to make a change. One person can say
something, but EVERYONE can make a difference! All I'm saying is YOU can
make a big imprint on the world by letting everyone know how serious this
topic is!"

In an editorial headlined "Just Do It . . . For 20 Cents an Hour," Max notes:
"While your thirteen-year-old daughter is buying a pair of Nikes, across the
world in Indonesia, a thirteen-year-old girl is sewing a pair of shoes, making 16

to 19 cents an hour." He continues, "Nike, whose namesake is the Greek goddess of victory, is an interesting title for a shoe company that exploits the labor of young girls." Max asks his readers to "open your ears and listen" to details of the working conditions endured by the young workers who make Nike sneakers: "Many of the tedious tasks involved cause blindness before the age of 25 . . . they work for two to five hours of overtime every day added to the nine hours of regular work. . . . Think of a prison. There are guards to make sure you don't leave . . . Women are forced to take birth control pills so their work will not be interrupted by pregnancy." His conclusion is a call to think and act: "Does free trade and globalization make it inevitable that some people have to live in poverty so that your son can be 'stompin' in his Air Force ones? Wouldn't you agree that it is Nike's responsibility to better the working conditions and wages of those who work for them? But since Nike CEO Phil Knight enjoys making over 5,000 times the months' wages of his employees slave labor, it is up to the consumer to continue to exert pressure on Nike. So, whose side are you on?"

William, in another editorial, asked: "Have you ever looked where your family rug came from? If it came from Pakistan, it was probably made with child labor. . . . Kids in Pakistan 4 to 14 years old are making rugs for minuscule amounts of money. The worst part about it is these same rugs are sold for thousands of dollars in the U.S." He describes the working conditions, noting: "The children do get fed, but it's only a small cup of tea and some pieces of bread. Can you work 13 hours with just that in your stomach and for just ten cents? I know I couldn't. . . . Why do they use kids and not adults? They use kids to make the intricate rugs because they have small fingers that can make small knots . . . the more knots per square inch in the rug, the more money you get. They also use the children because they say their eyesight is at its prime. They are also available and cheap and obedient after a few beatings." Concluding his editorial, he writes, "Is that rug worth the child's sweat, pain, or even death? I prefer wood floors."

Parallel Papers

One very nice extension or approach to the newspaper assignment involves creating a parallel paper representing another perspective on the topic under consideration. For example, if your class is studying the American Revolution, you can produce two editions, one published in Boston, and a second based in London. How might the two papers see the same events differently, and how might they report on them? You can complicate the matter even more by offering an edition, or sections of the paper, featuring viewpoints from rich and poor colonists, the Revolution as seen from Native American points of view, or expressing views from the communities of enslaved Africans living in the colonies. You want to help students to learn about point of view, to recognize that we have not always heard all points of view in the recounting of our history, and that there is not simply one point of view that encapsulates an entire society of people. You also want to stay sane—you can't represent all views all of the time. Balance is good.

The possibilities for this parallel processing are nearly infinite. You can focus on specific events, such as the U.S. Civil War (a paper from the North and one from the South) or the Vietnam War. In fact, there could easily be four papers related to the Vietnam War, with two based in Vietnam (north and south), one in governmental Washington, DC, and one from the midst of a march against the war. Various newspaper accounts of attempts to ratify the Equal Rights Amendment, or representing various sides from the situation in Cuba with the arrival of Castro to power would also serve to highlight the issues and points of view involved there. What would a newspaper published by refugees in Miami have to say about what has happened in Cuba and about what is happening now? What would a Havana-based, pro-Castro paper say about those same issues?

A class might publish a *First People's Times,* representing the point of view of first peoples in Australia, or in North America as they encounter those new to their shores and try to resolve conflicts over space and control. One class composed an edition addressing the environmental movement and the logging industry. *Animal Times* is a classic that was supposedly written, of course, by the critters that live in the woods, which differed quite a bit from the *Logger's Times* written by loggers interested in cutting the woods.

The purpose of the various editions is to present different points of view on controversial topics, and to further understand the role that point of view plays in determining what we know and how we know it.

Some Notes on Newscasts

Newscasts follow a very similar formula in that you serve as the editor in chief, you assign stories based on what you want students to research, and you monitor their progress throughout the process. Newscasts have their own technological and logistical issues, but today's videocameras are so sophisticated and powerful that they can produce good-quality video. You do, however, have the additional issue of editing. The following are four major approaches to this.

- A good deal of editing can be done within the camera. Just rewind and reshoot if you make a mistake, and shoot in the order that you want the broadcast to go. With a rehearsal or two before filming, this can work very well.

- A number of computers offer editing capabilities. Your school or district may have them, and also may have someone who can help you if you are not knowledgeable in this area. It does take a fair (or unfair) amount of time, so make sure you have the time.

- A third approach is from one tape to another, using two VCRs. You can record one segment from the master tape to a second tape, then find the next segment you want to use and cue it up before recording it onto the second tape. It is somewhat time-consuming as well, but not awful, assuming your newscast is to be half an hour or less.

- You can work in conjunction with a video production class (from your school or the community) and go whole hog. Class members can bring skills, equipment, and time to the project and can work in their studios, to match sound to video and add snappy fades and dissolves. It takes time and care to make the production really spiffy. This may seem excessive unless you are intentionally working on those techniques, or are working with a video class that is going to produce the newscast you create. This is a wonderful route if you can arrange it. Everyone wins!

Visuals: If It Bleeds, It Leads

Students who are creating a newscast have to make some decisions about what to actually present in addition to the image of a person reading from a piece of paper. What makes television news different from other media is the ability to communicate images, pictures, the drama of an emotional or exciting scene be it a roaring fire, a police chase, a ninth-inning home run, an interview with a grieving or joyous family member, a mind-boggling act of nature, or a particularly riveting speech. In fact, decisions about what to include on the evening news are often made based on the pictures that are available more than on whether it has importance or significance. It's why so many newscasts feature fires, car crashes and chases, and other sensational crime; they make good pictures. Around the newsroom they say, "If it bleeds, it leads."

Television shies away from stories that are somewhat heady, that require complicated explanations, that feature people sitting, talking, or, worse yet, thinking because those activities are boring to watch. Television decision makers are reluctant to do anything that will cause viewers to turn the channel, or to turn off the set. So, students have to decide how to deal with the visual elements of the stories they are reporting. There are several options; the limits are their imaginations, available equipment and expertise, the time they and you are willing to spend on the project, and the interest and skills of the particular students involved.

One option is to have your students role-play various scenes as they are being reported. They can conduct interviews with key players in the various stories, present reenactments of historical events (interviews of soldiers crossing the Delaware with George Washington, for example), perform excerpts from speeches made by newsmakers, or re-create ceremonies honoring or remembering people or events, and so on.

Students can create the scenes and either present them live or record them on videotape to be run as part of the newscast. Various stories can be recorded separately and then combined onto one tape in the order they will appear on the newscast. The weather forecast, the sports report, movie reviews, and various commercials can also be recorded separately and then placed on a tape in the correct order, or be placed on separate tapes and inserted at the right moment.

Another option can include having students find existing tape of events they are reporting on and offer that to accompany their reports. There are obvious limits to what can be done here since film and video are relatively recent, but there may be some scenes that will serve for some stories.

A higher-risk third option is to have everything happen live, with various actors playing out the scenes in question. Nothing would be prerecorded, or perhaps a few scenes might be. Most would be performed as the newscast is created. This approach takes some pretty thorough rehearsal of the various scenes and a well-disciplined group of performers.

A less dramatic fourth option is to have students create drawings or photographs that will claim the camera's eye as they read their various news texts. The camera can zoom in or pan across still photos or drawings, a la Ken Burns, as the reporter speaks.

Remember that the choices should be governed by the realities of the logistics (time, place, resources, student interests) and your objectives for the lesson. It can be very valuable for students to have to make choices about what to put in their newscast, and to select the images they will include to help either communicate the story or to attract and hold viewers, or both. And, of course, you want the students (newscasters and viewers) to have as much fun as possible while learning.

News Stories and On-Air Time
The time allotted to actual news on a national or local news program is minuscule. When time is taken out for sports, endless weather, fluff stories about treed cats and Spam-carving contests, news team chatter, and commercials, there is seldom more than ten minutes of actual news during a thirty-minute broadcast. The impact that this has on the news that we view is hard to over-estimate; it defines what we see, what we know, and what we never get to hear.

The average sound bite from the 1996 presidential election was approximately nine seconds long and, as of the 2000 election, it was closer to seven seconds. This means that when a candidate is talking, the clip we are shown is approximately seven to nine seconds in length, no matter how long the speech from which it comes, no matter how important the topic. How much context, understanding, or insight can a candidate bring to his or her viewers in nine seconds?

Sound Bite Activity

Ask each of your students to prepare a nine-second news story about something they really care about, telling the class what they think is really important about it. (*Note:* Assign this before you tell them that the average sound bite from the 1996 election was only nine seconds in length.) Make it clear that you will time them as they read and buzz them off the air after nine seconds, mid-sentence, mid-thought or not. Then do as you said. Give them approximately five minutes (or less) to prepare their stories and then go around the room, starting with those who are ready, and have them read their stories as you look at your watch. Buzz them at nine seconds and move on with no discussion.

Discuss the experience after several students have given their statements and ask them what it was like. Ask their classmates what they learned from the stories. There are some very simple questions to bring to the exercise: What could you include in your story? What did you have to leave out? How did you make the decision about that? Ask your students to speculate about whether audience members really understood what they wanted them to understand about their topic. Then, share with the class that this was the average time of a sound bite from the 1996 presidential campaign. They will begin to catch on to the limits of television news.

"In-depth reporting"—an extension

You can extend the previous assignment to the length of the average television news story, which is approximately forty-five seconds long. Ask your students to prepare stories about current issues (or past ones if you are studying long ago), again encouraging them to include as much complexity and detail as possible in the forty-five seconds. Proceed as before, sharing the frustrations and triumphs of these longer news stories.

Noam Chomsky was once asked why he was not on television news more, and he posited that some of the reason was related to the timing issues just explored. He said that if you say what people expect you to say they are not put off by, or confused by a very brief, headline type news story since they can fill in the rest themselves. If, on the other hand, you have something very unexpected or challenging to say, people are going to want to hear more, to understand why you are saying something so jarring, or why you are expressing such an unfamiliar or unpopular point of view. They may well understand what you have to say and why you are saying it if they are given the opportunity to sit with you for a significant amount of time, to hear your arguments and reasoning. Failing that, they may dismiss you as a crank or dismiss your arguments as ridiculous, unpatriotic, or scandalous. So news programs don't bring anything unexpected to its viewers because there is rarely time for those with the unfamiliar views to explain them. The structure does not allow it.

Magazine Show Format

Certain formats can take the time to explore an issue in more depth, such as news magazine shows (*60 Minutes*, for example), interview programs (*Charlie Rose*), or commentary programs (Bill Moyers' *Now*). It is on these shows that you are more likely to see challenging viewpoints that question the status quo. You might have your students prepare a news magazine or extended show on a particular topic, allowing them to really delve into the material and to fully present their ideas, questions, and arguments to a viewing audience.

Producing Radio Shows and Audiodocumentaries

Students can produce their own radio programming with the same focus and intention described for newspapers and television. They can produce talk shows that take place during the Revolutionary War, the Mexican War, the Great Depression, or at the time of the opening of Japan to the West. There could be music programs featuring music popular at various times and places. Sporting events from Roman times could be broadcast as twenty-first century events, complete with commercials, coaches' shows, and fan comment shows ("I don't think this current group of lions is as challenging as the group last year . . ."). The focus would be on learning about radio, about understanding what it does well and does not do well, and to understand more about what goes into decisions about what goes on the air and what does not (and the answer is always the same, no matter what medium).

Talk shows can be handled in class, with listeners (classmates) phoning in questions within the classroom as one or two hosts pretend to be on the air, or it can be done for real on student-run stations at the school or district level if you have that capability.

Mass Communicating—"A Powerful New Force"

There is a scene in the movie *O Brother Where Art Thou* that takes place on the doorstep of a lonely radio station, stuck seemingly in the middle of nowhere. Our heroes (a group of loveable, lower-class fugitives) are exiting the station, having just earned some money by singing a song "into a can." The fact that they have been recorded, without their knowledge, and that they will make thousands, if not millions of dollars for others, means nothing to them. They will eat this night.

The layers of irony are thick in this scene. The "Soggy Bottom Boys" have sung into a can and made big money for someone else as they spend another night in hiding from the law. The WEZY radio station is a dilapidated shack in the middle of rural Mississippi with no other human presence in view, and yet it is at the cutting edge of mass communication in this 1930s Depression Era scene. The station is a joke when thought of in our current context of mass media, but the station owner is truly in charge of what people in Mississippi (and elsewhere in the South) are aware of musically, politically, and socially. He likes the song so it goes out on the radio into the homes of thousands who have no other mass entertainment to pick from and little other access to the music made outside of their town. If he doesn't like the song, or genre, no one hears it.

The current governor of the state (Pappy O'Daniel), involved in a tough reelection fight, is heading into the station, and one of his entourage asks if he isn't going to "press the flesh, do a little politicking?" He responds with derision, "You don't tell your pappy how to court the electorate. We ain't one-at-a-timing here . . . We're mass communicating." "Oh yes," notes another, "that's a powerful new force."

WEZY is mass communication, and the governor, with his weekly radio show *(Pappy O'Daniel's Flour Hour)* sells his products (flour and his political career) to the masses. It is, relatively speaking, as powerful a voice for the *haves* of the time as today's media is in its updated, upscale format.

The issues of these scenes are still in evidence. Station owners still control what goes out on the air. Entertainment, moneymaking, politics, and control are still enmeshed to the point that it's hard to tell when one stops and the other starts. Mass communication continues to reduce personal communication such that politicians don't engage in "one-at-a-timing" behavior, choosing mass communicating to the tune of hundreds of millions of dollars for each election year, freezing out underfunded candidates who can't afford the mass communicating dollars.

We cannot hope to send our students into the world as responsible and active citizens without helping them to understand the ways that the media are owned and organized, and the ways that the media shapes the world in which we live and the world that we know. We must help students to become critical users of the various media they will encounter during their lives. The message throughout this chapter has been to encourage our students to understand how the media work, to become wise and wary users of it, and to pay attention, always, to the "man behind the curtain."

Resources

Bagdikian, Ben. 1992. *The Media Monopoly.* Boston: Beacon Press. Bagdikian was a reporter for the *Washington Post* and a longtime School of Journalism dean at the University of California at Berkeley. His book discusses how more and more of the media is owned by fewer and fewer corporations, and why that matters.

McChesney, Robert *(www.robertmcchesney.com).* McChesney is a significant media critic who helps to make connections between the various masters and roles of the media that were presented in this chapter. He has a website that introduces his books and many of the articles he has written. His insight is invaluable in understanding the complexity of the media as the source of the information–media as moneymaker contradiction.

Molnar, Alex. 1996. *Giving Kids the Business: The Commercialism of America's School.* Boulder, CO: Westview Press.

Postman, Neil. 1985. *Amusing Ourselves to Death.* New York: Penguin. This book really focuses on mass media and the ways in which it is compromised by its corporate ownership.

Selwyn, Douglas. 1993. *Living History in the Classroom.* Tucson, AZ: Zephyr.

Media Websites

These websites discuss, analyze, and critique the media and offer ideas for media education.

www.americanreview.net/whatsnew.htm
www.chss.montclair.edu/english/furr/media.html—MIT media criticism page
www.cursor.org/
www.fair.org/extra/current.html—FAIR
www.indymedia.org/—Independent media center
www.journalismnet.com/media/criticism.htm
www.medialit.org/—The Center for Media Literacy provides you with a wide selection of teaching tools, carefully evaluated for their quality and importance to the field. It is a national advocacy group for media literacy education; develops and distributes books, videos, teaching material.
www.medialiteracy.com/education/teaching%20resources.htm—A webpage designed for K–12 educators who want to: (1) learn more about media literacy, (2) integrate it into classroom instruction, and (3) make their students more media aware
www.rapidtree.com/mediacrit.htm—Rapid Tree
www.rougeforum.org—progressive education website—articles, links, essays
www.robertmcchesney.com/FavoriteActivistGroups.html
http://zena.secureforum.com/Znet/zmag/zmag.cfm—Z magazine (online)
www.zmag.org/—Z magazine

6

Picture This: Photodocumentaries

If I could tell the story in words, I wouldn't need to lug a camera.

—Lewis Hine

*T*wo distinct but remarkable experiences have shaped this chapter. The first occurred when I (Doug) was visiting my parents on the East Coast and was awake late at night, still living on West Coast time. I turned on the local PBS station and stumbled into "The Uprising of '34," a documentary about a massive strike of cotton mill workers that had erupted across the South in 1934. More than 500,000 workers walked out of the mills for more than a week, and seven were killed by National Guardsmen, their fellow townsmen, who had been called in to protect the equipment and the interests of the mill owners. This series of events was so painful to the residents of the town where the deaths occurred that they never talked about it, to their children or even to each other. It most certainly was not in the history books that I'd used in school when I was a student. The efforts of the filmmakers helped the people of the town in which the murders happened to discover their own history, to begin the painful and healing work of confronting their own dirty secret, as one of the townspeople called it. The film also served to help galvanize an effort to unionize the current factories in the town.

"The Uprising of '34" is clearly a documentary, a carefully and exhaustively researched film about a historical event, featuring many of the living participants (or their children) on camera, telling their version of what happened in their own words. The film is compelling because it is so clearly moving and

126

painful to those on camera, and because it tells the story of a major historical event (and tragedy) that most of us have never heard about. How could a strike of 500,000 workers, which resulted in seven deaths, not qualify as worthy of at least a mention in our social studies textbooks, or in our history classes? It was also remarkable to me in that many of the people telling their stories were not the types of people I was used to seeing on television, and the filmmakers clearly were placing them at the center of this work. These strong, plain-speaking, small-town, working-class people were trying to come to terms with a tragedy that had haunted them and their communities for sixty years.

It was clear that, in addition to serving as a fact-based documentary, "Uprising" had a clear and guiding point of view. The filmmakers had composed their work with a purpose in mind; they were using the film to encourage viewers to consider (and reconsider) union organizing in the small factory towns of the South, many of which are still right-to-work (nonunion) states.

I had uncritically assumed, especially throughout my school years, that something identified as a documentary is essentially neutral in its viewpoint and intention; most are made to relay the true story of something. In retrospect, that was clearly naive; "Uprising" called my attention back to the recognition that the creators of documentaries approach their work with their own knowledge, points of view, intentions, and understandings. They (and their work) are not neutral in approach, and their work isn't *the truth*.

The second experience came to me as the result of a most fortunate accident during my first year of teaching a fourth/fifth-grade class at Beacon Hill Elementary School. We were studying immigration, and the unit was going to serve as the backbone for a book, *Social Studies at the Center* (Selwyn and Lindquist 2000), which I was cowriting at the time. Judi Slepyan, a photographer friend of Tarry Lindquist, my writing partner, agreed to take photographs in our classrooms for use in that book. She was with us on a regular basis, got to know the students, and took pictures to the point that the students forgot she was there.

After a week or two Judi brought in some contact sheets and prints so that the students could see what she had been doing, and the room changed. The photographs of the children were beautiful—she is an extraordinary photographer. The students fell in love with the photos and began to see themselves in new, exciting ways. We made a book of these contact sheets and prints and students would spend their free time leafing through the ever-expanding class gallery, enjoying themselves and their classmates. They began taking themselves and the work we were doing more seriously and wanted to be the students that Judi presented to the world through her photographs.

At the same time, we were working with the photographs of others, trying to understand how photos tell their stories, and the ways in which a photographer can editorialize or guide viewers to understand the world in a particular way. The students learned about the choices a photographer makes while taking pictures, developing them, and the process he or she uses to choose and arrange the photos to be shared with others. We studied photographs, old and new, by photographers such as Lewis Hine and Dorothea Lange; watched parts of movies and documentaries; and watched and created commercials and advertisements trying to understand how the photos, images, and advertisements worked. We began to create commercials aimed at enticing potential immigrants to come to the New World (circa 1900).

At the end of the semester, we had created a book of "Coming to Seattle" stories, had read dozens if not hundreds of folktales, written some, and learned a great deal about our families and about immigration. We had also become inspired with regard to photography. The students were very excited by the book of photographs we had amassed, and of course by the prospect of seeing themselves in the published *Social Studies at the Center* book.

Their love of those photographs led us to a study of photography, with them as photographers rather than as subjects. Their interest was strong enough that they were willing to commit considerable time and effort to learning the skills of photography (see Figure 6–1).

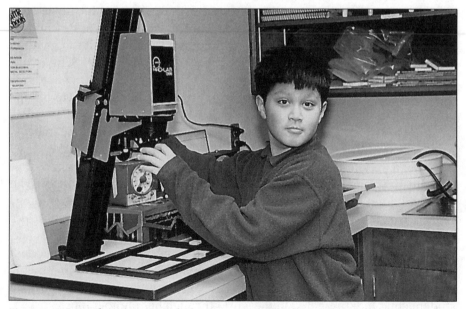

Figure 6-1 *Leung learning to use darkroom equipment.*

Our study of photography served us well in helping students learn about the documentary process. The students learned to appreciate the work of other photographers and to understand the stories they were telling, and not telling. They learned to *read* photographs and to recognize the photographer's point of view. Students learned how to create their own photographic stories, in individual photographs and in photo essays. Plus, they learned that there is no such thing as a neutral, unbiased documentary.

My students were able to bring their knowledge of how documentaries are constructed to the documentaries and movies we watched in class. We could discuss the choices the directors made, the points of view they brought to their audiences, and the ways in which someone might present the topic differently. The students became critical viewers, able to step back and to analyze what they were seeing. This is an essential skill for those growing up in our hyper-visual twenty-first century Western culture.

This chapter focuses on the photodocumentary rather than the video-documentary for three main reasons. First, the basic approach to creating a documentary is essentially the same, no matter what the medium. Working with simple cameras is very approachable for students (and teachers) of all ages and experience levels, and the learning applies to virtually any level of documentary making. Second, the materials for making videodocumentaries can be much more costly and out of reach for many classroom teachers, unless your district has editing equipment and videocameras. Third, I am not experienced at creating videodocumentaries, and would be hard-pressed to adequately describe the complex processes involved, especially editing.

In the Classroom

There is, of course, no better way to learn about the process of creating documentaries than by creating one, and this is the idea behind this chapter.

Much of what we know about the world comes filtered through someone else's eyes and lenses—a topic we've focused on in Chapter 2, I, Witness to History, and in Chapter 3, Lenses. We often see people and events of the world as someone shows them to us, and we are left with images that are experienced and accepted as *true,* that are shared by thousands or perhaps millions of *not-I witnesses,* to borrow Jan's phrase. We feel like we were there because the images are so powerful and clear, and we rarely think to question those images that we know all so well. The problem is that the images we know are often misleading, or incomplete, or only a small part of a much larger story.

University of Washington Professor Sam Wineburg gave a talk at a

Washington State Council for the Social Studies conference in the late 1990s about a recent trend he's found among this generation of students. Whereas past generations tended to learn about history from their parents or other family members, many young people today are learning their social studies content from videos and movies, including seemingly obvious fictions such as *Forrest Gump*. Dr. Wineburg said that this tends to be true even if they were watching with their parents, who presumably know more directly about the actual events portrayed and could (theoretically) offer correction or explanation to fill in the gaps in what they watch. The images are so powerful that they *become* true for the students.

This finding is of major concern to those of us who are attempting to help students learn how to learn about their world, to understand history and its relevance to what is happening in the world today. We are not simply dealing with a relatively ignorant and innocent population of young people who are ready to learn new information. We are starting with students who have been grossly misinformed in (to them) entertaining ways, which means we have to help them do a significant amount of *unlearning* before they can move forward toward a realistic understanding of why things are the way they are. In addition, we have to do this in ways that are genuinely engaging, and therefore memorable.

Although it is unnerving to think that we are competing with *Forrest Gump*, the challenge is not entirely a new one. Older generations also *knew* about the world through the media of their time. Previous generations mislearned about the West through television shows such as *Gunsmoke*, or the Wild Bill Hickok/Roy Rogers/Gene Autry formulas. We mis-learned about crime and the law through *Dragnet* and *The FBI*. We mis-learned about race through shows, such as *Amos and Andy* and *The Jeffersons*, and through the many different programs that featured people of color cast as criminals, servants, or as persons of comic or inscrutable natures. Lord knows we mislearned about women too. That they were moms in high heels and pearls; that they were helpless victims awaiting rescue; that they were temptresses; and, above all else, that they were pretty and thin.

Those violent and persistent images have shaped the world in their own manner, and we have had to labor against the weight of those stereotypes, whether they came to us on television, in the movies, in print journals and magazines, or through newspapers. As teachers, it behooves us to help our students to become critical and skilled observers of and consumers of the media, and to recognize both the way it shapes our cognitive concepts and the socializing role it plays in our lives.

Photodocumenting

In the collage activity described in Chapter 3, students focused on creating images to illustrate someone else's definition of history. In this unit students learn to select the images that will effectively communicate their own views of the world. Making these kinds of conscious and deliberate choices gives us the critical tools to evaluate the ways in which others manipulate us with their choices of images.

This chapter makes use of the process of photojournalism and the documentary to teach about the power of images and to recognize the influence and vision of the photographer or filmmaker behind the images on the screen.

What Is a Documentary?

As mentioned in this chapter's introduction, those making a documentary bring with them a particular point of view, history, and set of experiences that shape what they intend, what they find in their research, and what they present to the public. Individuals create their documentaries to make a statement, to say something. John Grierson, who coined the term *documentary* in a 1926 essay, said it is a "creative treatment of reality" (*NY Sun*, 8 February 1926).

Students (and teachers) can always help themselves to hold to the position of informed (and critical) viewer by approaching any documentary they view with questions such as the following:

- What do I see? What is here (without interpretation, without judgment)?

- How do I feel as I watch or experience the work? What is my emotional reaction?

- What does it remind me of? What questions do I have? What does it make me think about? Which parts of the work draw me in?

- Who made the documentary and what are their backgrounds?

- Who paid for the documentary? Where did the funds come from? What are the general policies and points of view of those who provided the funds?

- Who is featured in the documentary? Who is shown onscreen (or in photos), in what situations or contexts? What are they saying?

- Who is not featured or shown in the documentary? Are there points of view that are not featured or represented?

- Are there points of view that are not represented fairly, or in a balanced way? Why or why not?

- When was the documentary made? What has changed or come to light in recent years?

- What kinds of sources or reference material were used? Is there important research that was not included or given credence?
- Are there other works on the same topic that show different aspects of the subject?

Those making documentaries must wrestle with how to construct their work, given their own point of view, the information they have discovered via research, the limits and strengths of the media they are using (e.g., photographs, video, oral histories, theater, painting), and the characteristics of their intended audience. Students will learn best about these challenges to viewers of documentaries (and makers of documentaries) by creating them themselves. This will cause them to deal with the kinds of issues, questions, and processes dealt with by the photojournalists and filmmakers whose works they have been studying or viewing. Students will appreciate the work they are viewing and better appreciate the cautions and critical thinking they need to bring to the work as viewers.

The Steps

The process of creating a documentary, no matter what the form, includes the following steps:

1. *Choosing a subject or topic.* This can be based on any number of factors, including personal situation or condition, world or community factors, intellectual curiosity, or a particular element of timing or connection. However it happens, the subject is ideally one in which those creating the documentary have a real interest, and one that they have the resources to research.

2. *Identifying point of view, assumptions, and current knowledge.* Researchers are rarely starting at neutral with reference to a topic, and they should begin by identifying their beginning knowledge, assumptions, and questions so that they can plan their approach. They might ask themselves questions such as: Why do I want to know more about this topic? What do I think I know? How do I know it? How do I feel about it? What do I want to find out?

3. *Beginning the research.* How will you begin your research? Who might have something to say about this topic? Possible sources of information (including alternative points of view) include people, traditional reference materials, government records, libraries (public, university, and private), the Internet, and so forth. How will you locate this information?

4. *Amassing research with an open and critical eye.* What does each piece tell you? Where does it lead you? How does it line up with or contradict what you have found from other sources? What is missing from the story? What points of view are under- or overrepresented? What new questions have arisen from your work? How do you evaluate what you have found?

5. *Recognizing when you have enough.* When do you know you have enough information? How do you identify which possible new directions are worth pursuing, or which previous assumptions are being effectively challenged such that you have to go back and recheck your starting place?

6. *Organizing and evaluating your data.* Once you have decided you have enough information, how do you make sense of what you have found? What do you now understand about the topic? How do you organize what you have learned and what you now know?

7. *Selecting what you will communicate to others.* What is most important about what you now know? How can you best communicate it? If it is through photography, what choices will you make about the photos to include, the order to place them in, the captions or labels you will use? Which format will you use (book, storyboard, slides, overheads)? If you decide to make a documentary film or video, what will you show and how will you show it? What will you leave out? What do you want to communicate to your viewers and how will you do that?

8. *Checking for your attitude and point of view.* What role does your own personal vision and point of view play in this production? How do you choose to deal with that in terms of your audience? Are there other conclusions that could be reached based on your research? How will you address them in your work?

9. *Checking your work.* Is it accurate and effective? What impact will it have?

10. *Considering your audience.* What is the best way to reach them? Who is the audience for this work? How will you show your work? How will you learn from or build on the experience of showing your work?

11. *Assess the work.* What do you now know? How will you decide where to go next?

These basic building blocks, or steps, are valid no matter what form of documentation you and your students choose to utilize. You may choose to address them formally or informally with your students, but they are part of the process. In addition, the students will be most successful if they understand the forms of the media in which they are working so that they can make the best use of it. Which is to say, they should understand how to use a camera, how to develop film (a possible though not necessary option), and how photodocumentaries are put together, if that's what they are going to do. The next sections of the chapter include a basic overview of how to approach the use of photography as a documentary medium. It is very general because this is not the place or format in which to actually teach photography or darkroom work.

I also feel compelled to add that I began this process with very little experience with or an affinity for photography. I was learning along with (or just ahead of) my students, and often we discovered things together. I had good support in terms of a photographer who came into the classroom and found volunteers who helped in setting up and running the darkroom.

I found that there were many available resources within the classroom, school, neighborhood, and school district, plus members of the community who could support me to learn what I needed to know about photography and darkroom work. I assume that will be true where you live as well. There are some suggestions about where to look for help later in this chapter.

A Picture of Our Times

Photographs have played a major role in how we have experienced the world over the past one hundred and fifty years. There are famous photographers who have defined particular events or eras through their work, including Matthew Brady, Walker Evans, Dorothea Lange, Lewis Hine, Edward Curtis, Annie Liebowitz, Imogen Cunningham, Edward Steichen, Gordon Parks, and others. Their work has given us a sense of the times, fashions, issues, conditions, and "facts" of the famous and infamous events of our lives and our history. They have also communicated a feeling, an attitude, and perhaps some judgments about those times and events. Their photos were often an indictment of particular practices or states of being, an attempt to expose and alert the greater public to what was happening just out of their sight or awareness. The photographers listed here were not neutral, and their photos were not simply "Kodak moments."

Equally important are the hundreds (thousands) of *invisible* photographers who take the photos that appear in our newspapers, magazines, and journals; they are the ones that truly shape our notions of the world. They have shaped what we know of times past and present, and they offer both a window into times far from us in time and space, and a narrow lens that may mislead because of the slice they show.

Project Goals

Possible goals for a photography unit might include having the students do the following:

- Learn how to take pictures, to make use of a basic 35mm, point-and-shoot camera.
- Understand the choices a photographer makes about what to shoot, from what point of view, and for what purposes.
- Learn about documenting aspects of their lives, of telling a story about something that meant something to them, by creating a documentary sequence.
- Learn how to develop black-and-white photos in a darkroom; they would actually develop contact sheets and at least a few prints.
- Study the photographs of others and apply what they have learned to *read* the photos, for what they said, for what they did not say.
- Write captions and summaries of photos.
- Use photos to convince someone of something (persuasive writing).
- Look at photos in textbooks and history websites to understand more about various people, times, and places.

That's quite a healthy list of objectives; you need not reach all of them, but they do provide a clear direction for the unit.

Getting Started

Bring in photo books, from history, from the newspaper, from art books. All kinds of photo books can be easily gathered from most public library systems, or even from school district libraries, given enough advanced notice. Go through the books ahead of time to make sure those you hand out to students do not contain photos that are inappropriate for the students and the setting. Give students time to look through them with very little instruction or guidelines other than to notice what draws their attention, what they are attracted to, what they are repulsed by, what they find exciting, and so on.

Select three or four of the photos to use with the entire class. Make an overhead of a photo—black-and-white ones can be reproduced on an ordinary school copier such that most of the detail is retained. Color copiers can make relatively good overheads of color prints, though it is trickier, more expensive, and usually means going outside of school for the copies. I tend to use black and white for most group work, especially in the beginning.

Guiding Questions

Help the students learn to look at the photos by asking a few guiding questions:

- What do you see in the picture (without judgment or interpretation)?
- What draws your eye?
- What do you feel as you look?
- What do you think was most important to the photographer? Why do you think that?
- What is at the center of the photo? What is in the strongest light? What is in shadow?
- What is the point of view of the camera? From where is the camera looking?
- What are we not being shown? What would we see if the camera were focused in another direction, or from a different part of the room?
- What do you think the photographer wants us to get from this photo?
- What would be a good caption for this picture? Why?

This process might be carried out over two sessions, if needed. You are teaching the ability to make meaning from photographs, and it is a skill worth practicing enough so that students can gain the skills necessary to do so with any photograph they encounter.

Small Groups

Next, have the students work in groups of three or four to answer the same questions with other photos that you have copied and handed out—each group works with copies of the same photos. Stress that there is no *right* answer and remind students that they are allowed to respectfully disagree with each other. They should be expected to use specific evidence from the photos on which to base their opinions or observations. Have a whole-class discussion, following the small-group work, about what they found in the photographs and about the ways in which they approached their inquiry.

Taking the time to really look at a photograph, to spend thoughtful time with it, may be new to many of the students; it does take some practice. Give students the chance to practice this skill, to share their observations with others, and to ask questions.

Learning From the Masters of Photodocumentation

Students are now ready to examine the documentary work of photographers who have created a sequence of photographs in service of a point of view or to do with a particular topic. The process is somewhat similar to what they have just done with individual photographs. What is different about the exercise is that the photographer/journalist has created a statement composed of several photographs (and, perhaps words), presented in a particular sequence designed to tell a story, to make an overall point. The photographers were telling stories and creating a body of work that carries a larger idea. When they decided to take on the topic, a sequence of photographs was arranged in a particular order to create the desired effect on their audience. In the process, photographers make decisions about what to include, what to leave out, starting with what to photograph in the first place.

Two photojournalists who serve well in this role are Louis Hine and Dorothea Lange. Louis Hine, in his work documenting the exploitation of children in the workplace, for example, created a series of photographs communicating the experience and expressed his concern and outrage through his photos and text. Dorothea Lange told us stories about the Depression and the lives of migrant farmers struggling to survive. These Dust Bowl migrant farmers were largely invisible to most of the country and were rarely thought of by city dwellers who had their own issues and challenges.

Take a book, such as *Kids at Work: Lewis Hine and the Crusade Against Child Labor* by Russell Freedman, and have the students respond to the individual photos and the book as a whole. What is Mr. Freedman saying through the photographs he has compiled and ordered, and through his text? What is he not saying, or not showing? Are points of view missing, overstated, romanticized, or shown in ways that are misleading? How else might someone show the topic to create a different story, or to show the story in a different light? How is it different to see a series of photos rather than one shot, and what does that allow the photojournalist to do?

Students as Photographers

As students are learning to understand the ways in which photodocumentaries are constructed, they are also learning to take their own pictures, and then to create their own documentaries. The next sections offer some lessons geared toward helping students learn to work with cameras to create documentary sequences that tell a story. The sections are followed by the mechanics of making this kind of project possible (where to get materials, volunteers, financial support).

Working with the Cameras

It is best if every student has a camera, but working in pairs is okay too. I am assuming that the cameras you are working with are very basic, point-and-shoot 35mm, with few adjustment options. You can certainly use other cameras, including digital, but they are not econmical for most classrooms, so

138 · HISTORY IN THE PRESENT TENSE

I am assuming you will be going with the least expensive cameras for this lesson.

It is best to use black-and-white film, for several reasons:

1. The early photos students will be studying are black and white, and they can view their own photos in that same medium.

2. Most newspapers use black-and-white photos, which seem to be more authentic or real than color photos—an irony you can choose to explore with them (or not).

3. It is cheaper to work with black-and-white film, especially if you plan to set up a darkroom to develop the film yourselves.

4. Developing black-and-white film is relatively easy.

Beginning Exercises

First, of course, ask about experience. Many students (especially older ones) have taken their share of photographs, perhaps on much more advanced cameras than the ones you will have. After ascertaining students' experience levels, move forward with those exercises that seem most appropriate. Incorporate the expertise your students bring to this work; those with experience and comfort can share with their classmates, helping to support others, and working on ahead to expand their own skills and knowledge. There is some advantage to pairing experienced and inexperienced photographers, but that's not always the best for either. You might mix and match at various points in the process.

Give the students an assignment sheet with exercises designed to help students learn some basic principles of photography. The following are some exercises to consider:

• Give each student an empty frame for photographic slides (available at photography stores) and have them look through it. Have them *see* the world through this rectangle: How does the frame change the ways in which the world looks? How does the same scene look from different angles, from different positions, from different points of view? How does leaving out different components of a scene change the overall impact of what remains within the frame?

• Take photos into and away from a bright light source.

• Shoot at different distances from the subject, including very close and very far away.

• Shoot against a mirror or window where reflection might be an issue.

• Practice filling the frame, focusing so that the picture is balanced and doesn't leave lots of blank or empty space within the frame. Then see what happens if you leave a lot of space at the top or bottom of your frame, or aim so that your subject is really close to one side instead of at the center.

- Try taking a photo of the same situation from different points of view or angles, just to see how it changes the information contained in the picture.
- Take pictures outside in different kinds of weather, at different times of day.
- Shoot inside photos in different levels of and kinds of light.

Students should carry a small pad and pencil to record the details of every shot during that first roll. Light (bright, average, dim, natural, sunlight, fluorescent, whatever), distance, the detail they are experimenting with (shutter speed, if their cameras offer that option; flash or not; against a window; point of view). This record helps them learn from their attempts when the pictures come back.

This exercise can be tricky because you have to have a place to develop the film and a means to pay for it. It is most effective if you can get the pictures developed quickly so that students can learn from these first-roll experiments. Develop them yourself (or with help if available) if you have the means, or take them to a store that does developing.

Give the students time to look at their photographs; have them create folders (portfolios) in which to keep their work and their comments about it. The portfolios enable students to learn from their early efforts and to see their own growth over time. Writing information about what was tried and what was learned on the back of the contact sheet or individual prints is a useful step to take so that students can see why a picture was so washed out, overexposed, or hard to see.

Have the class members share what they have learned from this experimental work as a whole group. What have they noticed about what makes a good photograph? What are good things to remember when choosing to take a particular photo?

Storytelling with the Documentary

When you create a documentary, whether through photos or video, you are creating a story. A photojournalist has to decide about the same things one decides when writing a story: setting (place and time); main characters; particulars of the story; challenge or problem; ways in which problem is resolved or addressed; underlying theme; moral, or lessons learned; resolution (ending).

The photojournalist has to decide why he or she is creating the documentary, what impact he or she hopes to have on those who view the work, and how to create that impact. The photographer is creating this story or sequence for a reason, and an awareness of this purpose should guide the choices he or she makes along the way.

I have students tell their stories first in drawings, or in words. They have to tell about or show the main characters, the setting, the plot, the underlying theme(s), and the resolution of their story before they make their final selection and arrangement of pictures. They need to tell their stories to other people first, again in words, before they select photographs to tell the story.

I know others who do not use this approach because they are emphasizing the visual aspect of the photos, and I support that; photos carry information and an impact that words often cannot reach. I, however, do want students to recognize the story they are telling as a structure on which to make their decisions about which ones to include, in what order, and which ones to leave out because the photos do not help tell the story.

Students' Own Stories

The students are now ready to move into the next part of the sequence, which is using photographs to tell a story or communicate about something. A number of possible assignments could guide this learning; here is an example.

A Day in the Life

I ask students to practice documenting elements of their own lives. They might show us a typical nonschool day (or school day), aspects of family life, significant activities (teams, clubs, hobbies, friends), or in some way help us to get to know more about the world. They can take us on a journey from morning to night, or on a trip to a relative's or a friend's house. Students can show us various aspects of a hobby or activity they are engaged in, or take us along as they go to work.

They can introduce us to pets, siblings, or favorite stuffed animals. It's really up to them to decide what to share with us. The photographs in Figure 6–2 are taken from the work of one of my students who combined the mirror exercise with the day-in-the-life sequence; she and her mother photographed each other against the same mirror.

Community Landmarks

Alternatively, students might focus on a significant landmark or point of importance in their community. Their task is to help us understand the subject, about the reasons that it is important to them or to the community. It might be a supermarket, a boys and girls club, a barbershop or hair salon, the library, a community center, or a ball field; it should be a place that is important to the community for some reason and helps members of the class learn more about the ways in which it serves the community.

Figure 6–2 *LaToya and her mother took photographs of each other.*

I sometimes focus this discussion by sharing examples of various landmarks. Some are of national scope such as the Old North Church in Boston, Independence Hall in Philadelphia, or the Vietnam War Memorial in Washington, DC. Some are more local: Pike Place Market in Seattle, Gateway Arch in St. Louis, Fishermen's Wharf in San Francisco, Walden Pond in Massachusetts. Some are much, much smaller or unfamiliar: a particular barber shop where men gather to spend the day, or a beauty salon where women gather; a park where groups of people come to play cards or chess, or to sit and talk; a ball field where the community gathers to watch football games on Friday nights. The students' task is to define the landmark and to help us understand how and why it is important to the community.

Personal Choice

Another option is for students to create a photo sequence that helps us to know more about something that is very important to them. It might be an activity they are involved with, such as dance, a sport, religious group, tutoring program, or spending time with friends and/or family. Students choose the subject, which includes making sure that it is okay with others if they are to be photographed.

Have the students plan their approach, take photos, and then arrange the photographs on a large cardboard or lightweight posterboard so that you and other students can see them all displayed. They are to decide which photos to include (and which to leave out), what order to place them in, and what to say about each, via caption or explanatory paragraph, which involves looking at captions and how they function. How can you say just enough in a phrase or sentence to help your viewer understand the photos and what they are about? How do you decide what background or help others may need to understand the situation they are looking at since they don't have the background experience and information you have?

How to Share the Work

Have a gallery walk or tour for your class. Each student presents his or her photo sequence on a freestanding display board and you spend a certain amount of time simply looking at the work the students have done. You can either view the work together as a whole class, asking the students to talk about their boards as you come to them, or you can have students tour the "gallery" individually, noticing what they notice. Touring time, whether done individually or as a large group, is not a time for critique; it should be a very safe, low-stress, supportive environment.

Follow the gallery tour with a general discussion of what students noticed about effective ways of telling stories through photographs. What are the elements of effective displays? Which factors reduce the impact or effectiveness of documentary sequences? You can begin these discussions in small groups and then move to the large group or simply share as a whole group. Some questions students might think about while they are touring the gallery include those asked earlier in the unit: What do you see? What do the photos seem to be about? What captures your attention? What do the photos make you think of? What do they make you feel? What seems to be at the center of the photographs, in the best light? What do you think the photographer wants to communicate to you?

Social Action

You can stop the study at this point, knowing that the students have learned a great deal about presenting a story through photography, or you can take one more large step and have them investigate and communicate about some issue or situation they care about. I have had students document off-leash dog parks, dangerous and garbage-filled parks, bike trails that are not well maintained, dangerous intersections in their neighborhoods, the absence of resources for kids, and so on. We have also used the Internet to put together information about a topic of interest (child labor, for example), selecting photos taken by others and arranging them in an effective manner.

The ideal situation, in this reviewer's opinion, is to have students research something that truly matters to them, either alone or in small groups. The more they care about a topic, the more energy, resources, and attention students will bring to the search. There is sometimes an initial reaction against particular topics that seem, on the surface, silly or trivial (Barbies, baseball cards), but any study can lead to profound learning. Students will still be learning and practicing what they have learned in terms of research, documentation, and presentation.

City Council Testimony

One year my class was invited to take part in a citywide project linking kids and architects and the Seattle City Council. The idea was for the students to identify concerns about their neighborhood, from a kid's-eye view, and present them to the city council. We worked with an architect who helped us learn to use mapping skills, to *see* a bit the way an architect or city planner sees, and to assemble various data to make an effective presentation—to tell our story.

The students identified our school playground as an object of concern. This field, which doubled as a city park, was essentially a dust bowl that was often transformed into a mudpit for much of the Seattle school year. They noted that parks in other, more wealthy, sections of the city had grass, had better equipment, and were better maintained. We decided to bring this to the attention of the city council.

The students took walking field trips of the neighborhood, taking pictures. They photographed the field and play areas to show what was there (and what wasn't). The students decided to also photograph the neighborhood to show that there were really nice, interesting people who lived there and deserved a good park. The kids were afraid that the council members might not know who really lived in our (their) neighborhood.

The students worked in groups to compare and group the photographs they took, and then to arrange their work into a coherent and effective presentation. We talked through possible captions and narrative supports to the photos and had adults from outside our classroom look at the work to help us identify what was not clear.

Finally we presented our work to the city council, featuring text and captioned photos, student-written letters, and a blow up of the field at high tide (its very muddiest). Now, there is a grass field where the mudpit used to be—a wonderful legacy to the work of these students.

Milestones, Timelines, and Schedules

One of the most important logistical components to completing this project successfully is to be very clear about your expectations, about the dates when things are due, and about the reasons you have the timelines and schedules.

1. After a general introduction, each student or group of students chooses a topic to research and document. Part of the general introduction includes a classwide timeline, with due dates for various stages of the project.

2. Students develop and submit a plan for their project, which is due on a specific date soon after the assignment is given.

3. Schedule check-in conferences on a regular basis so that you can both monitor how the groups are doing and offer suggestions or guidance. I choose to require each group to submit their work for my signoff at each stage of their project development and research. I tend to be both flexible and strict about it, depending on the needs of the particular members of the group.

4. One of the stages in this process, mentioned earlier, is peer review. Each research unit (individual, pair, group) is required to share their work with at least one other group to receive and/or exchange feedback. This sharing happens at several stages of the process, and serves at least three functions.

- First, it encourages students to keep to a schedule so that they have something to share.
- Second, it gives the group practice in explaining what they have found and what it means, which gives them a chance to organize and critically evaluate the photos so that they can be ready to present them.
- Third, it gives each group a chance to learn from each other in terms of subject matter, research process, and presentation strategies.

Displaying the Work

Remember that one of the learning goals is to make use of photographs to document, to tell the story you want to tell. Be clear about what you expect in this regard in terms of number of photos, the role that captions should play, and the ways in which you want the displays prepared. The presentations themselves can be arranged and presented in many ways, including the following:

1. You can give each group a certain amount of time (say fifteen minutes) to share what they have found. Be aware that it is difficult to sit through more than a few presentations at a time, so space them out over a week or two. Consider giving extra points to those who present first, since they are "flying blind," without the benefit of observation. Throughout the process, I tend to have reflective conversations that focus on what is most effective in presentations as this is a learning process, but I'm careful to do so in a way that does not put down those who have not been effective.

2. You can offer the option of making overheads of the photos the group is using so that all will be visible to the audience. It is very frustrating to sit in an audience and be unable to see the photos, charts, and graphs being referred to during a presentation.

3. Have a museum-mode display, with each group presenting their work on a large board, photos and text arranged so that their content is self-evident and self-explanatory. Class members tour the room visiting each project board simultaneously, perhaps leaving one member of the group at "home" to describe or enhance what is presented on the board and to answer questions; this would necessitate having one-person research groups supported in some way.

4. Arrange to make presentations to other classes so that students can practice (and get the experience of) presenting to others.

5. Have everyone in the class research related topics, which are to come together in a public advocacy presentation of some sort such as the

presentation to the Seattle City Council concerning our school/neighborhood playground. This photodocumentary can still reflect student interest and concerns, but it should be centered on a guiding topic so that the class presentations will be coherent and focused. For example, students could research and document something having to do with child labor, or the experience of recent immigrant groups, or neighborhood beautification efforts, or resources for children. A general organizing topic still allows for many points of entry and focus for class members. A topic may have grown out of subjects you are studying as a class, or items students brought to class, which are taken up by the whole group.

One of my third-grade classes took on the topic of homelessness based on the concerns of a few students. The rest of the class embraced the topic and we investigated it as a class for months. One of my master's classes did common research on the subject of the coming of a new baseball stadium in Seattle and the impact its construction and existence would have on the community in which it was being placed. Our work on this topic included interviews of a wide range of people with something to say about the stadium, including shopkeepers, tourists, longtime residents of the area, workers who were being moved out of their worksite or laid off as businesses were forced to move, shoppers, politicians, homeless folks and street people who were being moved by the forces of gentrification onto another home turf, and various community groups. Students took photographs, visited the area at different times of day and night, recorded traffic patterns and volume, made drawings, and documented the area in any way they could. The students researched what had happened in other cities that had recently built new stadiums.

They also projected into the future, identifying those people they would like to interview again some years in the future after the stadium was completed. Students planned to take another set of photographs and conduct another round of interviews with many of the same people; of course, they had graduated and moved on by the time that came to pass. Even though they were not together as a class to do this future documentation, understanding the process and planning involved, at least theoretically, helped them to think about what was happening to the area.

6. Students could create a slide show, with a musical soundtrack, if desired. I worked with a master's student who wanted to know more

about the homeless teenagers who either lived on University Avenue in Seattle near the University of Washington, or who might as well have considering the amount of time they spent there. She did a combination of interviews, photography, and library research and asked the teens to document their own lives by taking photos. Karlie combined her overwhelming collection of data into a slide show with a sound track featuring music the teens listen to, the narration of factual information about homelessness, and observations made by the teens in their own, recorded words; it was stunningly effective. She did not pretend to be *objective* or responsible in a numbers sort of way—that was not her intention. She wanted to know more about the lives of the children spending time on University Avenue in order to be able to work more effectively with them. She did that and was very adept at sharing what she found with others.

Photographic Materials

There are some obvious material concerns with which you will have to deal, if you are having your students take pictures.

Photographs

There are many wonderful sources of photographs to use in helping students to learn how to view and to "interview" or question a picture. Many Internet sites offer historical photographs that can be easily downloaded, copied, and turned into overheads. The American Memory section of the Library of Congress is a huge site offering photos from different eras and historical contexts. *National Geographic* has a range of photos documenting the world in which we live, some from a disturbing or a controversial point of view. A very valuable discussion could ensue if you were to ask why *National Geographic* finds it acceptable to show native women topless when they would not do that with women in the civilized world. What does that say about the attitudes of the photographer and magazine? (I am not suggesting that you share these photographs of topless women in the classroom.) *National Geographic* magazine does have wonderful photographs of geographical features around the world, and they also have some very good historical photos that carry a great deal of teaching potential.

Art museum sites offer photographs from their collections. Independent media centers offer political news stories and photographs. Newspaper archives have vast collections of photographs as do state, county, and city historical societies and museums. Searching the Internet with a search term, such as "photo-essay," will offer many photos and photo sequences organized by topic or event, and doing so may help to enhance your selection for photographs to use in class.

Google.com and other search engines have an Images button on their home page. Clicking on this button gives you access to virtually all of the images that site links to; it is a relatively easy process to download those images. Check for permission requirements and restrictions; however, most do allow photos to be used in a classroom. An ordinary copier will serve your classroom needs if you are using black-and-white photographs.

Cameras

Finding cameras is your first order of business, which can be handled in a variety of ways. It is certainly possible to simply provide (or have students purchase) disposable cameras, and then take their work to professional developers. It is expensive (a new purchase for each roll of film) and will leave you without cameras once the project is done, but it is definitely the most trouble-free approach you can take.

I would suggest that disposables are not the way to go, for economic reasons because you are limited in the number of photographs students can take, and because you are then left without resources for next year's class. There are other options. One of them is to ask how many students have access to cameras from their homes. Many students do have their own cameras to use. I tend to shy away from this approach since there are so many things that can go wrong when cameras from home come into the room. They can be lost, stolen, or broken, and some students might bring in very expensive equipment. You can make a judgment about whether this is appropriate or not after consulting with the adults in your classroom community.

Getting and Funding Cameras for a Project

Very basic 35mm point-and-shoot cameras are relatively inexpensive these days. I bought a classroom set of Vivitar 35mm cameras for less than ten dollars each from a local camera shop three years ago. The shopkeeper was selling them cheaply anyway, appreciated the relative volume of the sale (nearly thirty of them), and wanted to support our educational efforts, which might produce future photographers who would buy more equipment from him.

Thirty cameras, even cheap ones, still represent a healthy chunk of change for most schoolteacher types, and mini-fundraising efforts make a huge difference. A number of potential sources of funds and cameras for this kind of project exist.

1. There are students within your classroom who can afford the cost of a camera, especially a ten dollar one. Every little bit helps, and they would presumably keep their cameras at the end of the project. Some students may willingly leave them for you, which means you'd have cameras the following year.

2. Local parent–teacher groups often allot funds for classroom projects. Your school may have an active PTSA, which has funds available for special projects, and is willing to support your efforts with a one-time allocation; you would then have a classroom set of cameras to use for years to come.

3. Various sources of money throughout school districts may be available to apply to projects such as this. The application processes vary, of course, and it sometimes takes some digging to find a grant that matches your need (into which you can fit your project), but there is often money that is waiting, unused. This can be a very good task to delegate to an adult who wants to volunteer in some way in support of your classroom; it does take time and some expertise and you are likely to lack at least one of those.

4. There are often grants available from the arts community programs, historical societies, museums, or other agencies that can be applied to this kind of project. If the grant requires a community-oriented project, or historical focus, for example, it might affect what you do the first year, but then you would have the cameras and can do what you want in subsequent years.

5. Cameras might be available through boys and girls clubs, other schools, or other sources from previous projects. Putting a note up in community centers and photography shops, in district newsletters, and at other public places might turn up donations of materials that were gathered for another project some years ago but have been collecting dust in more recent times. You do want to make sure that the donated cameras are in good working order. It is no blessing to receive free or inexpensive marginal equipment that ends up bringing massive frustration along with it.

6. You can simply buy cameras as a long-term investment. Assuming the worst, you have to pay $250 for cameras that will serve you over the course of your teaching career, or at least as long as they last; this is not a bad investment.

Digital cameras are wonderful for a couple of reasons: you can see what you have shot immediately, and you can easily download the pictures into computers to send via email or work with onscreen. They are, however, still very expensive to buy for one person, much less a whole class, and because of that it's difficult to let children experiment with them for fear of potential damage. This will change as the cost of digital cameras comes down.

Film and Paper Stock

You need more than just cameras to make this project go well, and this can result in unanticipated expenses that make life difficult for you and the students. Film seems cheap enough, but when you multiply needed rolls by the number of students you have, the cost adds up quickly. Then, you have to print that film, which again requires expense.

One possible approach is to include the cost of film and/or paper in whatever grant requests you are making. This would obviously be a requirement each time you do a photography project, but should be a recognized necessity to potential funders.

A second approach involves contacting photography stores, departments, or clubs. Many of them buy film in bulk and have massive quantities on hand. They might donate film or sell it cheaply because they believe in the project and can afford to help. Some may also have film available that is past the expiration date but still useable; this is especially true if you are looking for bulk film. The film may not be on rolls, ready to insert in the camera: it may need to be rolled onto reels that can then be inserted—a bit tricky and it requires practice. I would not suggest this direction unless you have skilled volunteers available to help, or are skilled at rolling film yourself.

The same general information applies to paper stock: photo stores, departments, or clubs often have paper/print stock that is out of date yet still functional. They will often donate such stock to your classroom or sell it to you for very little.

Darkroom

Darkroom setup is both very simple and very challenging. Finding equipment is much easier than you might think. Many people within and outside organizations, including schools and school systems, set up darkrooms with the intention of getting involved in it only to find that it wasn't what they expected, or that they were not interested in developing film any more for any number of reasons. So, there may be darkroom equipment gathering dust in bookrooms, on backshelves, and in garages and basements throughout your community. It is relatively easy to find equipment to borrow, to buy very cheaply, or to receive as donations; some may be able to take a tax deduction, though I've never pursued that angle. Many different online sites outline what you need in order to set up a darkroom, and members of the community are often available to offer support and advice.

One of the tricky parts of the process is finding a place to locate the darkroom. You need access to a sink, a place to install a safe light, and a location that can stay dark while you are developing film. Finding all of these is not always easy in a school setting. The good news is that it requires a very small area—we set up ours next to the sink in a small corner of the teacher's workroom in the back of our classroom pod. We arranged times with the other teachers who shared the pod and developed a clear communication system so that all knew when we could work, then went to work developing the film.

Volunteers

One of the most crucial pieces of a photography unit is having support, especially if you intend to develop film in your own darkroom. Support can range from having an extra adult on hand to supervise photography excursions to having help in loading film, to having someone to work with the students as they develop film. You can't easily supervise darkroom work while you are teaching the class, and it is best to do darkroom work with one or two students at a time, so you have to make some logistical choices. I usually stay with the class while knowledgeable volunteers work in the darkroom with one or two highly motivated students, which is a good setup.

So, where do you find these volunteers? Many places. Here's a brief list: adults in your own classroom community, in your school community, at a local college or university, especially a teacher training program in which prospective students need a certain number of classroom hours as part of their entry requirements; through a photo class or club; at senior or community centers, especially those that offer photography classes; through experimental or community schools; through notices placed at photography stores; and your own network of friends. Many people have experience with photography and like to work with children. You might also find volunteers who are less comfortable with children but are willing to help put bulk film on rolls or will develop many rolls of film when you need a quick turnaround. It does take time to structure your classes to make the best use of willing adults, but it can be done and is well worth the time spent in organizing the experience.

Videodocumentaries

The first step to take in learning about videodocumentaries, as it is with photodocumentaries, is to view the work of others, to learn about how documentaries are made. I offer students some guiding questions to bring to their reviewing, and solicit questions to add to the list from class members. The following are some sample questions:

• What are you seeing on screen? No interpretations here, just who or what is on the screen and what is happening?

• What seems to be (or clearly is) the topic or subject of the documentary?

• What are the filmmakers saying about the topic? How are they making their case?

• Which images are most powerful and most important in the film?

• Which points of view, which voices are underrepresented or left out entirely?

• Who is paying for the work? Who are the sponsors or producers?

• In what ways do the filmmakers backup what their work presents? Is this a fact-based presentation? Where are they getting their facts and are there questions about those facts?

• What are you reminded of as you watch the film? Does it match or contradict what you already know about the topic? Does it remind you of anything in your own experience?

• How does it make you feel? Are there things that make you feel strongly, one way or another, as you watch?

• What questions does the film raise for you?

• Are there other takes on the topic that might organize and present information in a very different way, leading to other conclusions?

These are some clear reminders that students should always have with them as they watch:

• There is no such thing as an objective film or documentary. The filmmaker always has a point of view, a way in which he or she views the topic. Every shot, every piece of audio and video in a documentary is included as a result of a decision made by the filmmakers.

• The events as portrayed on the screen may or may not have happened in the order they appear in the video. To make the viewing coherent, even historical footage may have been combined in a way that does not reflect the actual order of events. Also, the manner in which material is combined or edited can produce a very particular emotional or intellectual reaction.

• Many documentaries offer stock footage in places that show a scene something like what must have happened rather than the actual event.

It may not damage or lessen the credibility of the work, but it isn't absolutely accurate.

• It is not always obvious to younger viewers, or even some older ones, that documentaries that purport to show scenes from the American Revolution or the Civil War are fictionalized accounts, showing what might have happened. They show the characters having invented conversations, taking positions and attitudes about past events as if you were watching them exactly as they happened. It's fiction dressed up to communicate a historical truth or point.

• There is always more information that was gathered and filmed than what you see. The filmmakers choose to include what they do for artistic as well as content-based reasons. There is always the question of what they left out, and the reasons for what they left out.

• The views presented in videodocumentaries are those the filmmakers chose to present.

Making Videos in the Classroom

Many of the same principles apply as outlined in the photography section. First the students need to learn to use the cameras, practice documenting something that involves little or no research (just to practice the process of documentation), and then move to combine research with documentary filmmaking as a sequence. They can document the same kinds of subjects as described in the photography section. Equipment issues are likely to be more significant, and it may be necessary to structure more work during the school day using school equipment. Some families are likely to have video equipment, and recognizing this might help in determining logistics. A few students may be able to carry out the assignment at home, but others will need time at school, either supervised by volunteer adults or working with you after the school day is complete, or through some other arrangement.

Possible Assignments

The same kinds of assignments that lend themselves to photodocumentaries also lend themselves to videodocumentaries. Students can use video to show a typical school or nonschool day in their lives. They can introduce us to their families and/or friends, to hobbies and activities and teams, to aspects of their school experience. They can focus on particular landmarks or significant elements of their community or neighborhood. Students can pick a particular issue that is of concern to them, be it a dangerous intersection, or a strip of bike path in need of repair, or a neighborhood that offers no opportunity to its children. They can focus on a larger issue, such as child labor, war/peace issues, resources for the poor, or whatever draws students' concern and interest.

The steps for creating the video work are essentially the same as were outlined in the beginning of this chapter, with the additional challenge of editing the video. This is not the place for describing the editing process and how best to deal with it. Suffice to say that there are resources in virtually every community to assist with video production, and it would serve you well to find out what is available to you where you are. Community groups often have video production and editing classes. Universities, colleges, and community colleges generally have classes that are open to community members, as do some school districts. Many larger cities have community access networks that offer various media classes and options.

Learning to See Changes Us

Documenting the world we live in is an act of scholarship, an exercise in paying attention, and a means by which students can begin to enter beneath the surface of the world. The material in this chapter barely scratches the surface in describing the process of helping your students to take a "creative approach to reality," as John Grierson (1926) phrased it, to become careful, attentive, communicative actors. There are dozens of other processes for helping students learn to see and to share what they have seen, including (in addition to photography and video) collecting oral histories and creating documentary theater (see Chapter 7, Making History), writing, painting and drawing, composing, theater and scene study, and focused research such as the product research described in Chapter 4, Trading Stories.

One who is engaged in documenting the world with the intention of gaining an understanding and perspective that will enable him or her to communicate about what has been found will be forever changed through that engagement. Once a student has documented her day, she will never live in the same way again. Once that student has researched and communicated the story of the shoes she wears or the soccer ball she kicks, she will bring that awareness to all of the steps she takes during the rest of her life.

Resources

If You Have the Time . . .

Museum archives are a wonderful source of photographs. Newspapers and libraries also have archives of photographs. Used book stores are an excellent source of books and magazines containing photographs. Household collections are also amazing treasure troves. Families often have boxes of photographs that span a century or more of history. They are incredible conversation starters, and an instant link between personal stories and the larger history that we ask students to learn.

Technology Is Your Best Friend . . .

If you have access to the Internet, you have access to vast libraries of photographs and photodocumentaries. Begin with a search engine such as *www.google.com,* which links to websites across the Web. If you type in the term "photograph," "photodocumentary," or "photo-essay," you will be offered thousands of site options housing photos. You can also click on the Images button on the Google homepage, which offers an even more direct link to the Web's photographs.

Books

Freedman, Russell. 1994. *Kids at Work: Lewis Hine and the Crusade Against Child Labor.* New York: Clarion Books.—A photodocumentary about child labor and those who brought that practice to light in the early twentieth century.
———. 1987. *Lincoln: A Photobiography.* New York: Clarion.
———. 1983. *Children of the Wild West.* New York: Scholastic.
Grierson, John. 1926. "Flaherty's Poetic Moana." *New York Sun.* 8 February 1926.
LeGuin, Ursula, and Roger Dorband. 1993. *Blue Moon over Thurman Street.* Portland, OR: NewSage.—Photographs and commentary on a journey in Portland, Oregon, from one end of Thurman Street, in Portland, Oregon, to the other.
Menzel, Peter. 1994. *Material World.* San Francisco: Sierra Club.—A look at the ways people live around the world.
Selwyn, Douglas. 2000. *Social Studies at the Center.* Portsmouth, NH: Heinemann
Stanley, Jerry. 1994. *I Am an American.* New York: Crown.—A photodocumentary of the Japanese American internment.

Websites

http://chnm.gmu.edu/fsa/—Photodocumentary of the Great Depression, featuring photos of Walker Evans.
http://dir.yahoo.com/Arts/Visual_Arts/Photography/Documentary/—Yahoo's site, which offers presentations of photodocumentaries, photo-essays, and other visual arts presentations.
www.fotoessay.com/—A website featuring photographic essays on various topics; requires previewing as not all images are appropriate for all students.
www.globetrotter.berkeley.edu/Ewald/—A site dedicated to the work of Wendy Ewald, who has done extensive work teaching photography to children. She has a number of books and articles devoted to the topic; much of the material is referenced on this site.
http://memory.loc.gov/ammem/amhome.html— American Memory, the photography collection at the Library of Congress, is the best place to start. It offers a staggering number of photographs by some of this country's most famous and skilled photographers, gathered by theme, era, and topic.

www.nationalgeographic.com/photography/—*National Geographic* photography essays, documentary photography tips, and links to photographers' websites, photography education, and photojournalism.

www.pathfinder.com/Life/lifehome.html—*Life* magazine's online version; the print version of *Life,* available in virtually all library archives, is a wonderful source of photography through the years.

http://vads.ahds.ac.uk/vads_catalogue/jrcal_description.html—Documentary Photography: Jacob Riis; a multimedia CAL program to teach the analysis of documentary photography.

http://xroads.virginia.edu/~UG97/fsa/welcome.html—Discussion of Walker Evans as a man who revolutionized documentary photography. Features some of Evans' photos.

7

Making History

That's what being young is all about. You have the courage and the daring to think that you can make a difference.

—Ruby Dee

One evening in early December 1999 we stood on our front porch and listened to the pops and whistles of rubber bullets and tear gas canisters being fired in the distance. Earlier that day, we'd joined throngs of peaceful demonstrators to express our concerns about the many issues raised as a result of agreements made by the World Trade Organization (WTO). The Third Ministerial of the WTO had come to Seattle, bringing trade ministers from more than 120 countries, representatives of well over 700 Non-Governmental Organizations (NGOs), and an estimated 30,000 to 50,000 demonstrators. In addition to massive street demonstrations, there were rallies, forums, debates, and teach-ins all over the city.

The news leading up to the Ministerial had focused on the many issues that the WTO's presence raised: free trade versus fair trade, genetically modified foods, endangered species, national and local sovereignty versus WTO agreements, and labor standards around the world. Once the meetings and the demonstrations around the meetings began, media coverage switched from issues to focus on disorder in the streets of Seattle.

Alarmed at the images on their nightly news broadcasts, friends and family called to make sure we were all right. We assured them that the bulk of the demonstrations earlier that day had been peaceful, and that we had not been involved in any of the considerably smaller ones that led to property damage and harassment of WTO Ministerial attendees. But once the sun went down, after we'd gotten back home, the situation had begun to deteriorate. While the ministers conducted their sessions inside, tear gas filled the air outside, and rubber bullets and billy clubs were used on dozens of protestors, the overwhelming majority of whom had remained peaceful.

Although many of these protestors had openly announced their intentions to interfere through nonviolent direct action with the "business as usual" of the WTO, it seemed to have taken our mayor and police force by surprise. Initially, the police responded by trying to disperse the determined demonstrators without mass arrests, but the tactic seemed to have backfired. To regain control of the downtown area, police ranks drove the protestors into more residential areas, and city officials declared a "no-protest" zone to keep demonstrators at a distance from trade ministers. This rekindled the protests, as concerns about First Amendment rights grew. By the end of the week, more than 500 protestors had been arrested. Lawsuits stemming from these arrests would not be settled for nearly two years. The WTO meetings proceeded, but the ministers failed to reach agreement on a number of issues. One thing on which they did concur: The next meeting should be held where it would be less accessible to demonstrators.

History was in the making. Teachers everywhere took advantage of it.

Students As History Makers

This chapter focuses on the dual aspects of making history. The first is participation in events themselves. The second is the recording and interpretation of those events for audiences, both contemporaries and posterity. In this activity, students create their own record of history based on research that includes interviewing participants in current or recent historical events and also include their (the students') own participation in events. They determine their editorial point of view, select salient details, edit and arrange the material into documentary theater. The basic format suggested is that of readers' theater, in which the focus is on reading a script rather than fully producing it. To enhance the theatricality of it, however, other elements are brought to the production such as background music, songs, short memorized scenes, slides, and/or video projection backdrops. We also present a variation of the process, which models the development of a play in the more commonly seen format of characters in action in a setting.

A Word About Documentary Theater Projects

Theater is by its very nature a collaborative art. Few classroom teachers are familiar with every aspect of theatrical production. If you are among this majority, you need not despair. There are several ways you can coordinate documentary theater projects with help from your students, your colleagues, parent volunteers, artists-in-residence, and community arts agencies. You can also learn by doing. For those who would like to take the plunge, this chapter contains some tips, basic definitions, and suggestions for how to identify topics to make it easier for you to help students research and create their own theatrical accounts of history.

The Steps

The steps to use are slightly different in focus than those outlined in Chapter 6, Picture This. There is a larger scope here—so multiplicity of point of view is both an explicit part of the research and a part of the consideration of choosing the final production elements. In other words, rather than one student artist expressing his or her own point of view, there is representation of many points of view in a readers' theater documentary.

1. *Identify the topic.* On large sheets of butcher paper, list guiding questions. Students should circulate and write in response to the various cues. What do you know or think you know about the identified topic? What do you want to know? Who do you think would be interesting to interview or find information about and why? Which points of view would we need to know to have a rounded view of this topic?

2. *Compile a list of research resources and interviewees.* Base the list on the information identified in 1. The items can include people to be interviewed or researched. If they are local, write letters of invitation asking if they would be willing to be interviewed, preferably in the classroom so that the whole class can participate; otherwise, a team of two or three students can do the interview. If they are not local, identify research methods for finding out what they are saying—watch newspapers for relevant articles; watch television news; do an Internet search; find out if the person in question has published any articles, books, or other statements.

3. *Research and interview.* Resources also include books, articles, videos, and other documents and documentaries that provide background information. Research can be as direct and contained as reading some contrasting short articles and opinions, or it can be as in-depth as taking weeks or months to explore many resources. The amount of

time devoted to this phase will vary according to your overall goals, and the time available in your teaching schedule.

4. *Transcribe the interviews and compile research data.*

5. *Edit the material and arrange it.* Write up a first-draft script. This may sound like a daunting task, but it needn't be. The project examples in this chapter will provide some detailed guidance and structure for how to do this.

6. *Consider what is missing and how to find it.* This is the point at which it is important to review the group's initial sense of the scope of information they want to have. It's also the time to revisit the question of editorial point of view. You'll need to look at what has been gathered thus far, and see if the information meets the editorial concerns of the students in terms of breadth, number of *voices* represented, and so on.

7. *Fill the gaps.* Do additional research or original writing. Often, this is an excellent time to schedule some creative writing tasks; students can write individual or group poems, character monologues, songs, skits, and scenes for consideration.

8. *Finalize the working script.* Add new material and revisit step 6. Were the concerns all met? Is the script telling the story according to the agreed-on point of view of the students who are producing it?

9. *Rehearse the script.* This may be an excellent time to collaborate with your school's drama department and/or discover the talents of some of your students; others can serve as student directors.

10. *Perform the script for an audience.* This is a short, simple sentence, but it implies making quite a few decisions. Who is your audience? You may want to limit it to a performance for the class next door. You may want to schedule performances for several classrooms or the entire school. You could go beyond that, arranging one or more performances that will be open to the public or tour in other schools in your area.

When Opportunity Knocks

There are times when you will find history on your doorstep, and the whole world is watching. At Cleveland High School in Seattle's Beacon Hill neighborhood, teacher Faith Beatty recognized an opportunity to bring history into her language arts and drama classrooms. The WTO provided perfect grist for the mill; its meeting had recently concluded amid tempestuous demonstrations, citizen hearings, and sensationalized news coverage.

Faith knew that some Cleveland students had attended the demonstrations, and others had lost income from part-time jobs they couldn't get to because of the turmoil in downtown Seattle. Many of them also had classes with teachers who had attended the demonstrations. All of them had seen the televised images when things turned ugly—riot police in full gear, demonstrators choked with tear gas, looters carrying off coffee from Starbucks, broken windows, and trashcan fires.

Faith brought in artist-in-residence consultants—John Sullivan, director of Seattle Public Theater's Theater of Liberation troupe, and me (Jan) to help her. Our task was to collaborate with her and her students to design a project that would connect essential language arts skill-building with the important social studies content that was inherent in this historic event. The students were going to make some more history. One of the students had already been involved directly with making the history of the WTO; now all of them would be engaged as historians documenting the event through their research and interpretive efforts.

We started with large sheets of butcher paper, labeled with guiding questions: What is the WTO? Who is affected by the WTO? How are you affected by the WTO in Seattle? What questions do you have about the WTO? Who are the people you'd like to hear from about the WTO? The sheets were hung around the room, and students circulated, writing whatever came to mind in response to each prompt. We also generated a list of countries represented by the clothing and household items that we either had in the classroom or at our homes. (To those who've read Chapter 4, Trading Stories, this is a familiar exercise.)

The list was impressive; from a class of fewer than thirty students, we generated a list of well over thirty countries, without even trying: Angola, Austria, Bangladesh, Belgium, Bolivia, Canada, Chile, China, Colombia, Costa Rica, France, Germany, Great Britain, Greece, Indonesia, Italy, Ireland, Israel, Japan, Korea, Lesotho, Macau, Malaysia, Mexico, Pakistan, Peru, the Philippines, Poland, Russia, Sri Lanka, Switzerland, Thailand, the United States, Vietnam, Zimbabwe. Clearly, our lives are very much affected by international trade. In the context of this particular project, we simply generated the list and posted it as part of our discussion of the interconnectedness of all countries and peoples in the world.

The lists on butcher paper gave us a beginning point for putting together invitations to guest speakers. In class discussions, we fleshed it out. Some resources were very close at hand, indeed. In Faith's first-period class, there was a student who had been at the demonstrations; two teachers in the school had participated as well. All were invited to be interviewed by the students.

Students also wanted to hear from someone on the host committee who'd invited the WTO ministers to meet in Seattle and someone from the Port of Seattle about the effects of world trade on our city. They wanted to hear from someone representing the point of view of labor union members who had demonstrated, someone who knew something about fair trade issues, someone who could speak on human rights issues. Students wanted to hear the story from the point of view of the police. They wanted to know what it was like to face so many demonstrators, and what it felt like when they were ordered not to stop the few who were vandalizing stores. They wanted to know about the crowd-control weapons, devices, and agents the police had used. They wanted to hear from reporters who'd been in the thick of it. They were curious about the so-called "Eugene anarchists," blamed for the window-breaking and other acts of vandalism that had occurred. They wanted to understand the legal status and authority of the WTO. Students would have liked to have heard from trade representatives, particularly those from smaller countries, but they had gone home.

While Faith arranged for students to videotape the interviews, her students wrote letters of invitation to individuals and/or agencies that had been identified as having information of potential interest. Ultimately, eight individuals accepted invitations to be interviewed by Room 120 students: a member of the carpenter's union, the student and two teachers (one a biology teacher, the other a horticulture teacher), a representative from the Seattle Host Organization, a King County Worker Center staff member who had a close vantage point at her office window from which to watch some of the demonstrations and arrests, an attorney with particular expertise in police accountability and crowd-control methods, and a human rights activist with the Free Burma Coalition. The students were disappointed that no representative of the police department could come to the class; because of the number of pending lawsuits against the police, they were unable to make any public statements. The police department did, however, provide students with a great deal of written material on policies, procedures, and the preparations they'd made for the WTO events in Seattle.

The trade delegates' points of view were also ones that we would have to research through printed materials and other forms of documentation rather than interviews. The journalists' experiences and points of view would be derived from watching videotaped news reports and reading editorials and news articles. The legendary anarchists—or at least some of them—had posted their manifesto on the Internet, which gave us at least one anarchist point of view to explore.

To prepare for their role as interviewers, the students read contrasting articles about the World Trade Organization. One was in favor of it, the other was critical. They charted the pros and cons, and this joined the gathering display of student-generated questions, topics, and concerns on the walls of the classroom. They also viewed videotapes that gave them an overview of some of the issues involved: *Showdown in Seattle (www.indymedia.com), Voices of the WTO* (TVSEA), and *One Child's Labor (60 Minutes)*. The last features Craig Kielburger, a Canadian youth who, as a twelve-year-old, launched and still leads an international campaign of children to combat child labor (see Chapter 4, Trading Stories).

Based on the readings and their very fresh memories of news coverage of (or personal experience with) the demonstrations, Faith and the students worked out a number of questions they wanted to ask each interview subject to get things started. Interviewees were asked a little bit about their own background; what they thought of the WTO; what role they played, if any, in planning for it, managing it, or protesting it; and what they thought the major issues were. To keep the conversational ball rolling, each question was assigned to a particular student in the class, but students also had practiced how to follow up on questions. When a speaker said something that interested them, students could ask questions to elicit responses of greater depth and specificity. As the interviews were conducted, they were video- and audiotaped. (The guests signed releases giving permission for their words to be used in a play to be developed by the students and for their entire interviews to be stored in archives.)

The next task was to transcribe all the interviews, a very time-consuming task. We'd anticipated this and had created a line item in our budget for paying a typist to transcribe all the interviews. We could have had students work on this in keyboarding classes or asked for parent volunteers; however, in this context, we needed to be sure the material was transcribed accurately and in a timely fashion, so it was deemed an appropriate, even necessary, expense to get it done quickly and by paid labor. Funds came from a small grant that we'd secured to underwrite the cost of the project. When transcription was done, we had approximately twelve hours of interviews, comprising some eighty or so single-spaced pages of text.

It seemed like quite an overwhelming challenge to reduce all those words into eight monologues representing the eight interview subjects, but it really wasn't that difficult to do. In Faith's first- and second-period classes, students worked in teams to read through one or more interviews and circle the parts they found most compelling or interesting. A second round brought two or three more sets of critical eyes to each transcribed interview. I have used this technique in several similar projects and the results are always the same. The students generally have good instincts for what to excerpt. They know what caught their interest when they first heard it, and they know what will catch the interest of their eventual audience. Figure 7–1 shows a sample of a page of transcript, with passages circled by two or more students. Sometimes, if I think there's something that is interesting or important that the students haven't selected, I'll circle it so that it will be included for consideration during the next step.

Barbara Hazzard, interviewed by students in room 120, Cleveland High School, April, 2000 on the W.T.O.

against it. But, you know, some of the people that were protesting had very specific issues that they felt very strongly about. What was interesting is again from the media's perspective - and I don't want to sound like I'm anti-media, because I'm certainly not - maybe in some ways with the media we get what we deserve - maybe we're not getting better media because we're not demanding better media.. but the media sort of represented the protesters as all being of one voice, whereas there was a lot of differences. I mean, some of the protest groups, labor, for example, they were huge. They were like 30,000 of the protesters on Tuesday. Labor wasn't saying, "Let's get rid of the W.T.O." I mean, sometimes a rank and file member would say that. I mean, I saw a journalist on Saturday…like, just a union marcher. "Why are you here?" "Well, we need to get rid of the W.T.O." But actually what the labor leaders were saying is "We want the W.T.O. to also handle international labor law. That's not something the W.T.O. does at this point in time. There's another international organization that does that. So here was, you know, 30,000 people; but what they really wanted was to have the W.T.O. take on more responsibility. Where, there were some protesters on the street who really felt we'd be much better off if there was just no World Trade Organization at all. So, you know, I think for some people who feel very strongly about something, then yeah, get out there and have your voice be heard. But it was unfortunate that all the voices were just sort of lumped together, and so there was not really any messages that were clearly heard.

Now, it's interesting on the labor issue, U.S. labor feels very strongly that W.T.O. should be handling labor issues with trade issues, and that's something that President Clinton was also proposing, and you know, a lot of the U.S. business community was saying, "That's fine, if everybody else wants to go along with that, that's just great." But the thing about the W.T.O. is that 135 countries get together and have to decide something by consensus. Which means everybody's supposed to agree. Well, the developing countries said "No, way. You know, the only reason why you want to tack on labor to this is so you can discriminate against our products." So, again, the protests, you know, were -- it was interesting, reading in the paper this week, they were saying "Oh, the D.C. protesters weren't successful in shutting the meetings down like the Seattle protesters were." Well, in reality, the meetings would have failed if there hadn't have been a protester on the street or not. And a lot of it was because of that labor issue, because the developing countries were saying "No way. You are just trying to discriminate against our goods." And there was also the issue of agriculture, which was very complex as well. And so, it's interesting that now the media is kind of rewriting history, and giving - you know, saying the meetings failed because of the protesters when in reality there were just issues within that convention center that there was no way they were going to get resolved in four days. So, it's never a bad idea to protest. I guess I'd like to hold the media more responsible for really protesting about what the issues are, and I think that the protesters…just last week on the radio, somebody who was protesting against the World Bank was saying "It's my constitutional right to prevent them from attending that meeting." I thought "well, wow, I've read the Constitution and, you know, you have the freedom of speech, but don't those people who want to attend that meeting also have freedom of speech?" So I would disagree with the protesters there, where they felt they were some sort of ═ there was a right that they had to prevent people from attending the meetings. Those people have rights too. And those people's rights were really trampled.

Figure 7–1 *Editing goes quickly when several readers circle key phrases.*

This technique allows you (the editorial collective you) to sort through an enormous amount of material fairly quickly. At the same time, the students who are reading/editing are reviewing the content. So you (the teacher) are achieving two very different but very important goals with one activity.

The excerpts from our WTO interviews sorted themselves without too much trouble into responses to several guiding questions, which were arranged in a logical chronology: What is the WTO? Whose idea was it to bring the WTO Ministerial to Seattle? Who came? Why were they here? What were the issues? What about the Constitution? What role did the media play? What comes next, both in terms of the WTO and the local Declaration of Civil Emergency? Looking back on it all, was it worth it? These questions were distilled into a series of slides that would provide transitions from one part of the script to the next.

This part of the arranging was something John Sullivan and I did, bringing our sense of what would make for an onstage presentation of the material that an audience could follow easily. I have found that there are phases of these sorts of projects in which it's important for me or the classroom teacher to make some decisions and present them to the students. Sometimes the students accept the decisions; sometimes they choose to amend them in various ways, from small to large. In this case, they agreed that we'd fashioned a workable sequence out of the material. We now had a first working draft of the monologue material that would form the backbone of the Readers' Theater docudrama, which the students would eventually perform. (Later in this chapter, I'll discuss an example of how a project developed when the students didn't like the teachers' proposal.)

Still missing was the point of view of a police officer. Students applied the same editing process as they had to the transcriptions to the written materials sent by the police department to create the character voice of a police officer; that point of view was added to the play. Also missing was any voice that was seriously critical of the demonstrators. Editorials, mined for main ideas and paraphrased, gave this reportorial point of view. As with the police voice, it was integrated into the basic structure.

Our next task was to read the draft through and discuss what was missing. As interesting as the interviews had been when the guests were in the room, we knew that nine or ten interwoven monologues in and of themselves were not going to make compelling theater for an audience, so we added two more elements to our working script. I don't actually remember whether the suggestion for video elements came from the students or from the teaching team. The nature of these projects is that ideas are bandied about and the good ones tend to take hold and grow, while the boring or inappropriate ones tend to die on the vine. At any rate, we concurred that some video would really help our presentation. The Independent Media Center, which had produced the "Showdown in Seattle" video, which documented the protests, granted us permission to use portions of it as backdrop and transition images. In addition to being visually interesting, the material we selected added more points of view and more background information for the audience.

Several cast members form a tableau: an image of protest in the streets. GUY 1 and GUY 2 look really bored.

GUY 1:   What's on t.v.?

GUY 2:   Dunno.

GUY 1:   Okay, let's check.

GUY 2 mimes turning on the television, and they both lean forward in interest. Videotaped images appear on the large screen over the stage of the WTO protests. The tableau comes to life, adding to the images on the screen.

TV VOICE: And tonight's story is . . . the WTO!

GUY 1:   Geeze.   GUY 2: (overlapping)   Damn it!

GUY 1:   Isn't it over yet?

GUY 2:   What the hell is WTO, anyway?

The actors in the street image, GUY 1, and GUY 2 return to their seats as Host Committee Representative (HCR) and Reporter 1 (REP 1) step forward to talk to the audience.

HCR: President Clinton thought it would be a good idea to host the WTO in the United States.

REP 1:   And Governor Gary Locke wrote in the November 29 Seattle Times, "This historic event will change the course of international relations in the new millennium and will also leave a positive impression of our state for many years to come."

VIDEO IMAGE: a montage of WTO events: gas, flames, people running from police, tanks, etc.

AKSON steps forward and talks to the audience.

AKSON: I'm like you guys. I was like "Oh, I don't think it's going to affect me, oh, man, this is some boring news story." Then I learned it was some real stuff. It'll affect us.

Akson, HCR, and 1st Reporter focus on the other cast members as they say these headlines:

LATIA: Debt of Poor Nations Should be Cancelled, Religious Groups Say

KAO: In a Shrinking World, Trade Represents Choice

TYRA: World's Poor Will Lose if Union Agenda Accepted.

ANGIE: Human Rights, Big Business Intersect on WTO Stage.

WHITNEY: Indigestion at the World's Dinner Table

ROSIE: One WTO, but Many Factions

JOSH: Must Trade Rule the Planet?

SLIDE: Who's Idea Was It?

1st Reporter: (to Host Committee Rep) Whose idea was it to bring the WTO to Seattle?

HCR: Government people, business people, and civic leaders decided this would be a great meeting for Seattle to host: a high-level, international meeting, so it would get good international press exposure.

Figure 7–2 *Putting it all together into a working script.*

Still, there was a need for more interaction between the live characters on the stage. We wanted to observe and respect the reality of each of the guests having been in conversation with the class, and not with each other, so we decided against cutting and pasting their words as if they'd been in debate or discussion. Instead, John worked with the students to improvise transitional scenes, and the students and I then scripted the ideas that worked best. This gave us an opportunity to explore even more points of view in the script: passersby, businesspeople affected by the demonstrations, anarchists, police officers facing demonstrators, demonstrators facing the police, delegates.

In the actual events, as in any large street demonstrations, chants and slogans were prominent. Some of them were incorporated into these little scenes to provide a sense of the event and to function as transitions between the Readers' Theater monologues and the scenes—"Fair trade, not free trade!" "Ain't no power like the power of the people 'cause the power of the people don't stop!" "The people, united, will never be defeated!" Plus, the chant that would become the title of our play, "The whole world is watching!" Finally, we had our working rehearsal script (see sample page in Figure 7–2).

As we rehearsed, we kept our collective eyes and ears open to the intention of the project—to have a number of voices heard and to respect the deeply felt differences of opinions. This had been a strongly felt and expressed value of the students from the very beginning. The class included student activists, but it also included students who identified more with the businessowners and police points of view than with that of the demonstrators. As a group, the students didn't want their production to have any particular spin. They wanted to make the point that the existence of the WTO raises very important issues and that each person needs to become informed and to make his or her own decisions about these issues and how to respond to them.

One theater form that provides a sense of closure and captures the complexity of a number of character points of view is called a *fluid sculpture,* and that is how the piece ended. One by one, characters step downstage and pick a motif line from something they've said earlier, accompanied by a motif gesture. As each character joins the sculpture, she or he dominates it briefly in volume, then drops to a level that allows the next voice to be heard. When everyone is part of the picture, they listen carefully to each other and tune in to the group as a whole, allowing their voices to mingle before fading out and coming to a still, single tableau of the cast, representing multiple voices and multiple concerns. In our final tableau, it was a line spoken by Barbara Hazzard of the Host Committee that became everyone's statement: "Think for yourself."

The play was performed for other students at Cleveland High School, and for parents, neighbors, and members of the larger Seattle community (see cover of playbill in Figure 7–3). The student who had participated in the demonstrations was the only member of the cast who actually played himself. Many of the people who'd been interviewed were able to attend the evening performance.

The Fringe Benefits Are Not So Fringe

Drama projects are inherently multiple intelligence theory in action. Aristotle pointed it out centuries ago, and it's still true: drama engages us through poetry, song, story, movement, visual impact, and emotion. Every drama

Figure 7–3 *Artistically inclined students can help with program and publicity art.*

project I've ever been involved with or heard about generates stories of students who are finally, suddenly engaged in learning; of students who make important breakthroughs in terms of their ability to work with others cooperatively; of students who amaze everyone by displaying talents no one, perhaps even themselves, knew they had before. A drama project is inherently cooperative, inherently kinesthetic. For the student who does not learn easily in the modes most favored—linguistic and logical/mathematical—a drama project can be a profoundly different experience of school, one in which the student can demonstrate a depth of learning that is undisputed.

In our WTO project, there was a student who, through no fault of his own, had ended up in the honors section of the language arts class. He was a special education student, but needed the credit for graduation and had no other time available in his schedule to take the class. During the interviews, he was thoroughly engaged, and asked many questions of our guests. It was the first time he'd become a real part of the class. Prior to the WTO project, it had been difficult for him to fit into the class as a whole, and he had tended to tune out. After the interviews, he continued to participate fully.

Another student, the one who had attended the demonstrations and was interviewed by his classmates, emerged as a real leader. His classmates began to look to him not only for his firsthand accounts of what had happened in the streets, but for his understanding of the background and implications of the events. Several others learned to overcome their basic shyness and performed admirably on stage, composed, effective, and audible.

All the students were affirmed by the very enthusiastic and appreciative responses they heard from audience members. These are the fringe benefits of doing such a project that are actually very central to this kind of teaching and learning.

Flexibility Is Our Motto

I promised to say something about what happens when the students don't care much for the suggestions of the teachers. In these situations, it is important to be guided by that underlying commitment to starting with the students and their concerns.

In 1998, Faith, two other Cleveland High School teachers, and I collaborated on a labor history project, also rooted in oral histories. Students in language arts, social studies, and keyboarding classes interviewed a wide range of people in the community about their chosen professions. They distilled the transcripts into excerpts that caught their interest the most, as described before. I put them into an initial draft of a readers' theater script, and Faith and I presented them to her drama class.

This was a new group of students. In retrospect, it is hardly surprising that they were not enthused. They hadn't been part of the interviews, hadn't asked questions, hadn't reviewed and edited the transcripts. Nor had the students been part of the earlier exploration of labor history that involved making collages (the activity described in Chapter 3, Lenses) or the discussions of labor and of oral history techniques. In short, there had been nothing that allowed them to connect with the project yet. They wanted to have much more of a hand in fashioning the play. The interview segments as such, they asserted, wouldn't make very interesting theater. They wanted to perform in a more traditional play, with characters who would interact with one another.

The students were right. The interviews about jobs were interesting reading to those students who were considering pursuing the same careers as the interview subjects. But they were likely to be less engaging to a *regular* audience. Okay. So it was back to the drawing board, with not much time in the schedule. One lively class discussion of brainstorming ideas for how to be faithful to the content (labor history and labor opportunities) while telling the story in more dramatic terms led to an inspired suggestion: a parody of *A Christmas Carol*.

Some students didn't know the Dickens story, so during the following class session I reviewed the basic structure. Soon we had identified the hero of our play: Evan Ebeneezer Scrooge, a disaffected student in a labor history class. Evan Ebeneezer falls asleep during class and is visited by the Ghosts of Jobs Past, Jobs Present, and Jobs Yet to Come—the structure was perfect. The Ghost of Jobs Past could speak to the history aspects, the Ghost of Jobs Present could include some of the information and issues from the interviews, and the Ghost of Jobs Yet to Come could allow the students to express some of their career goals. Of course, for Evan Ebeneezer, the Ghost of Jobs Yet to Come would be a guide to the frightening spectre of unemployment and lost opportunities. By the end of the play Evan would be glad to wake up and take his education seriously.

During one class session, we outlined the basic episodes: An opening scene introduces us to Evan cadging spending money from his hardworking mother. In the second scene, Evan falls asleep in class and is visited by the Ghost of Jobs Past who takes him and his best friend to see a bit of the coal mining history of the area and a glimpse of the Great Depression. They see their great-grandparents on opposite sides of a strike, and Evan's grandmother selling apples while his grandfather is asking the famous question, "Brother, can you spare a dime?" In the next scene, the Ghost of Jobs Present shows Evan that his mother is dealing with sexual harassment in the workplace, and his father is torn between his interest in joining a carpenters' union and his fear of losing his job. Finally, the Ghost of Jobs Yet to Come shows Evan a future in which all his classmates—even his fast-talking buddy Jobless Johnny Johnson—have become happily and gainfully employed while he has become a penniless panhandler. Evan awakes a changed man and goes on to host a Labor Fair in which the students present what they've learned about labor history at an evening assembly.

In another class session, students broke into small groups and we tackled writing the scenes. I wrote the basic scenes needed on the board, and asked for volunteers who had ideas about how one or the other of them might unfold. We quickly built the groups this way, so that each student was working on the idea that most appealed to her or him. I circulated among the groups and asked some guiding questions to keep students on track. Most often, the question was simply "What happens next?" or "What does the character say next?" If students are stuck with that form of the question, I make it a little more open ended: "What is one thing that might happen next?" or "What is one thing the character might say next." Usually, the first thing that comes to a student's mind in response to that sort of question is a viable idea. Following it through a couple more rounds of questions very quickly exposes whether it truly is viable. If it's a dead-end, and the student says so, the next question is simply "What would happen instead, then?" Most of the basic script was created in that one class session.

A young woman with some experience and interest in theater became the student director for the class, and under her guidance, the cast improvised around the basic scenes to make the language more realistic and add their ideas. (Faith reports that this student, who once was struggling in school, is now in college pursuing a teaching certificate. She intends to teach social studies. These are the stories that keep us going, aren't they?)

Meanwhile, the excerpts of the original interviews were not tossed. We made a pre-show tape of selected segments from the interviews. While the audience was waiting in the lobby to be seated, they could hear the bits of interview and view the collages other classes had created. The students edited the excerpts further to distill extended quotations from them, and these were included in the program.

Inclusion

This story illustrates one of the very basic principles of creating theater from work done by the students. The more student voices and suggestions you can include, one way or another, the more students will *own* the project. By the time we'd finished producing "More Than a Paycheck," more than a hundred students had participated in some way. Is it work? Of course. Is it worth it? Absolutely. As soon as a student finds his contribution excluded from the project, he will have little incentive to stay attached and focused. The families of students, too, will be more interested in a project when they know their sons and daughters have an authentic part to play in it.

Breaking the Silence—The Japanese American Experience

The year 1992 was a significant anniversary for a lot of people in the United States. Most will recognize that date as the five-hundred year anniversary of Columbus's voyage to find India, which landed him instead in the New World. (Of course, there was nothing particularly new about it to the indigenous inhabitants who'd been here already for perhaps tens of thousands of years. For them, it was the uninvited visitors from Spain who were new.)

It was also a significant date for Japanese Americans: 1992 marked the fiftieth anniversary of Executive Order 9066, which resulted in the dislocation of 120,000 people of Japanese descent, most of them citizens. They were ordered from their homes and communities and taken to assembly centers, then to internment camps.

Bobbi Morrison, a teacher at NOVA High School in Seattle, and Nikki Nojima Louis, a playwright whose work is based in oral histories, set out to create a semester-long course that would look at Twentieth Century America by focusing closely on the experiences of three generations of Japanese Americans. I (Jan) was invited to join the project as a curriculum consultant to help plan the sequence of lessons and activities. Later in the semester, I returned as a theater artist-in-residence to help the students shape the material they felt was the most important to communicate into a docudrama.

In this project, the immediate connections to the lives of most of the students in the class were perhaps less obvious at first, though there were two students of Japanese descent in the group. So we began the project by having students create fictional characters: members of a typical 1938 Japanese American family. For a more detailed description of this process, see the Creating Characters chapter in *Living History in the Classroom* (Selwyn 1993).

Working with construction paper and guiding questions, students made the faces of a father, mother, four children, and a grandmother. Nikki shared information with them both about traditional Japanese names and the penchant that immigrant Japanese had for naming their American-born children after famous U.S. presidents or other prominent figures. The students named each of their characters accordingly. They all had traditional Japanese names, but the children had American names as well. Throughout the semester, we would check in with the family members to consider how each might be reacting to historical events, as well as design creative writing and art projects that engaged the students in exploring their own feelings and experiences.

The steps in the project were much the same as in the basic unit outline at the beginning of this chapter, with a heavy emphasis on the research phase. Most of the semester was spent doing in-depth study of the topic, including the following:

- Reading and discussing fiction, nonfiction, plays, and historical documents, including *No-No Boy, Nisei Daughter, Farewell to Manzanar,* "Unvanquished" (a play by Holly Yasui, daughter of one of the key figures who resisted internment, Min Yasui), "Breaking the Silence" (Nikki Nojima Louis' play based in historical research and oral history), and *Divided Destiny: A History of Japanese Americans in Seattle,* Supreme Court briefs, and the official letter of apology from President George Herbert Walker Bush that accompanied reparations checks
- Engaging in role-playing activities such as exploring the arrest scene from *Farewell to Manzanar,* adapting a chapter of *No-No Boy* to stage format, and reenacting a Supreme Court session considering constitutional issues
- Completing arts-based assignments such as creating the faces of a typical Japanese American family of the late 1930s and designing floor plans for accommodating a family of four in a 20-by-20 cubicle
- Viewing videos such as *Chrysanthemums* and *Unfinished Business*
- Interviewing members of the Seattle community who lived through the experience of life in an Internment Camp
- Writing creatively—for example, creating sensory-awareness poems of assembly centers, writing tanka poems, and writing reflections on being in two worlds at once as were young Japanese immigrants who were straddling the traditional world of their family and the culture of their new country
- Learning the basics of taiko drumming

As with the WTO project, when it came time to edit a semester's worth of discoveries into a single one-hour presentation, the students were very adept at identifying the crucial elements they wanted to include. It took one class discussion to arrive at the following list of what they felt was most important:

- Statistics and historical background
- The immigrant experience
- The disruptions to the lives of people who were interned
- What life was like in the assembly centers and camps
- Supreme Court cases that grew out of resistance to internment
- The redress movement
- Current status of redress payments

They wanted to include their own writings, as well as excerpts from some of the literature they'd read. The chronology of historical events suggested the structure for the play. All the material they'd read and written was put together in a notebook, and we made two or three sets.

Another class session was devoted to the editing process. As in the WTO transcript editing session, students read through and circled what they felt should be included. We created a second packet, with just the circled material, and went through the process one more time; otherwise, we would have had to stage a four-hour marathon instead of a fifty-minute performance! This netted us our basic working script.

Most of the students in the class took roles as actors in the production, while one or two preferred to work on backstage aspects of the performance. Three of the students studied taiko in greater depth, and opened the play by performing a piece composed by Masaye Nakagawa, who also instructed them in the art of taiko drumming. The play was performed for a number of other high school audiences. One performance was open to the public; for that one, three members of the local theater community joined the students.

A Word About Music

Readers' Theater can be a somewhat wordy, boring affair if you don't observe the audience's need for changes in the rhythms and energies of the performance at hand. Music, in my opinion, is an essential ingredient for moving something from the realm of informative but dreary into the realm of compelling theater. Where do you find appropriate music, either for the students to perform as part of their play or for transition and mood music (which is called *incidental music* in the world of professional theater)? It depends, of course, on your topic.

When we put together the play on labor history, there were collections of labor history songs that we drew from, but there were also the songs we knew of ourselves. From my own youth, I recalled the song "Get a Job!" I found a CD that included it, played it for the students, and they agreed that it was the kind of upbeat sound we needed to transition from our prologue into the main part of our script. For pre-show music, "More Than a Paycheck" by Sweet Honey in the Rock introduced some of the themes the play would consider and helped put the audience into an attentive mood. It also inspired the students to title their play after it.

At two points during the play, students sang little bits of some famous songs about labor (or lack of it): "Solidarity Forever," the sort of unofficial anthem of the organized trade labor movement, and "Brother, Can You Spare a Dime?" the unemployment lament from the days of the Great Depression.

But the students wanted something that was more their own music in the play as well, so four of them wrote a rap song to be the finale. The song had a melodic refrain, which reinforced Evan Ebeneezer's insight: "What's coming from your past? Your future's out to get you; make it last!"

In "Breaking the Silence," the students began the show with taiko drumming, a traditional Japanese drumming form that they'd studied as part of their semester-long curriculum. Shakuhachi flute music accompanied the early narrative lines about immigration statistics, and other snippets of traditional Japanese music underscored scenes and provided transitions.

In "Where We're Coming From," a play that resulted from an interdepartmental exploration of social issues among students at Nathan Hale High School in Seattle, the students worked with composer-in-residence Suzanne Grant to create original songs. Additionally, there was traditional Cambodian dance music and African drumming to accompany the choreographed dance pieces that opened the show.

Music is important beyond the fact that it covers transitions and reinforces conceptual ideas. When the text is difficult to listen to, either because it is long or because it is emotionally challenging, music provides a relief and release. The most difficult emotions put to music are transformed and somehow more manageable. Music hath charms, whether to soothe the savage breast or the restless audience member, and the more we can incorporate it into teaching and learning experiences, the better.

Multiple Payoffs

As educators, we are constantly faced with the need to plan *backward*. Standards, frameworks, benchmarks, and lists of outcomes all tell us what we are expected to ensure by way of student learning. Thinking about the outcomes we want to effect helps us focus our attention in two (at least two) ways. First, we have to think about the discreet steps needed to get from where we begin to where we wish to end. What skills do the students already possess? What information do they already have? What do we want them to be able to do, express, discuss, evidence as learning by the end of a particular lesson or unit? Second, we have to organize our own knowledge about the lesson or unit at hand, and think about how to select appropriate details and communicate effectively what we know about a subject. In this process, we must move to those "higher-level" thinking skills that Benjamin Bloom calls "synthesis" and "evaluation." However, the process will only be truly successful if we also have the "lower-level" basic knowledge foundation in the content area. How can we select the most important details if we don't have a larger body of knowledge to begin with? The payoff for us is that by engaging in this process, we solidify and articulate our own learning.

Projects that culminate in documentaries give students an authentic way to experience this same benefit. The collective knowledge of the students has to be large in order for the final product to represent deliberate artistic and editorial choices. And the production of a theater event, or videodocumentary, based in the students' inquiry into a theme or topic, brings the unit of study, whether it is the WTO or a topic from ancient history, into the present tense for students.

I'm Inspired, Now What?—Some Rules of Thumb

If reading this chapter has convinced you (or reinforced your conviction) that you'd like to guide your students in creating a theatrical event to focus their learning, the following are a few ideas about identifying subject matter:

- Look for thematic connections between your basic curriculum and the headlines, such as movement of peoples, conflicts between nations, exploration, human impact on the environment, empire building, cultural change and/or conflict, the interaction of culture and technology. These are the kinds of themes that tend to run throughout recorded history, and even prehistory.

- Look to significant anniversaries of historical events: the quincentennial—500 years after Columbus; Executive Order 9066—fifty years later; fifty years of the United Nations; a hundred years of flight; the Lewis and Clark expedition; the centennial, or sesquicentennial, or bicentennial of your own community.

- Consider problems or issues in your classroom and/or school community; conflicts between groups and cliques; the experiences of newcomers; dating relationships, tolerance issues.

Make sure the learning experiences you design allow students to gather enough information so that they have numerous points of view to contemplate, something to edit, something to whittle down, something to weigh and consider. Be sure that you've designed it in a way that the students have authentic input. This doesn't mean that they are the sole determiners of the curriculum content, but it does mean that it is a collaboration between teacher and students to shape a project the size of a theatrical presentation. You are all going to spend too much time on this to make it be something that doesn't have full buy-in.

Speaking of Time

Once you have a script, if you are aiming at a script-in-hand readers' theater presentation without any bells and whistles, you can probably get something put together in as few as a couple of rehearsals. If, on the other hand, your goal is a finished production, in which the actors have memorized their lines and are playing out scenes rather than reading monologues, you can figure that for every minute on the stage you'll need to invest at least an hour of rehearsal. No kidding. It's roughly the same formula for videodocumentary (i.e., for every minute of finished video, you'll probably spend at least an hour in the editing process). If you've got any technical aspects whatsoever to your production, your last two to three rehearsals will be more about ironing out the kinks in your light and sound cues than about polishing the performances.

Most projects fall somewhere between these two extremes, requiring a few hours of rehearsal to present a polished Readers' Theater piece. It's important to know how to estimate the real time requirements accurately so that you don't try to accomplish too much in too little time. Otherwise, you'll be frustrated and your student actors won't be able to do their best. I think it's better to do a fifteen-minute piece well than to do an hour-long piece not so well.

Full Production?

If you are aiming at a full production, be aware that students who are new to this kind of work will resist the notion that they will need to put significant time into preparing properly. They'll think they can wait until the day of the show to memorize lines. Do everything you can to head this off. Set a deadline for being off-book that is well ahead of your production date and attach real consequences to it. No matter how talented an individual is, it's not responsible to the group for him to put off deadlines and wait until the last minute to prepare. Help students understand that the reason they will be wonderful on stage is that they will be so prepared that even if something happens at the last minute, they'll be able to deal with it. Rest assured that things will happen at the last minute: a cast member will fall ill or be suspended for an unrelated event; a parent will suddenly move out of town, taking your lead with her; a student who works a part-time job will suddenly have her day off rescinded.

If you've prepared them well, this is when the remaining students in the cast will really shine. They'll rearrange lines, reassign parts, rewrite scenes, rehearse madly in the wings, agree to do things they never thought they were capable of (like singing in front of an audience, or taking on a lead role). Students will help each other be ready for their cues backstage, and onstage they'll pick up a line for a rattled colleague. They'll find out that as long as they do it all with confidence and poise, their audience will never guess that anything different was ever supposed to happen.

One little trick I've picked up over the years is to promote the play as a script-in-hand reading if you've any doubt whatsoever that you can get a full production together. Then, if you're able to take it further, the kids look great. They were only expected to read from a script, and here they are with their lines memorized!

Skills for Readers' Theater Formats

If you decide to do a project that involves more than your student actors reading their scripts from seated positions and you don't have a drama teacher to take on directing responsibilities, you'll need to teach students a few simple vocabulary terms and concepts, just to be able to efficiently direct traffic onstage. If you do have a drama teacher or theater artist-in-residence to help, that person will also need to teach these concepts. Your familiarity with them will help you support that colleague. A few of the basics are defined in this chapter's glossary.

If you've chosen to go the simpler route of having your actors sit in a semi-circle of chairs or stools and read the script, you'll still probably want to spend some rehearsal time practicing picking up the cues. You also may need to attend to sitting and script-holding postures and to page-turning techniques. Encourage your actors to sit tall, with their scripts held lower than their faces. Novice readers and shy students sometimes hide behind the script, which makes it very difficult for the audience to hear them and impossible for them to be seen. Turning pages creates noise, so everyone should turn pages quietly and carefully at the same time so that they don't upstage whoever is reading at that point.

Unless you've got a state-of-the-art theater with built-in amplification, at least some of your students undoubtedly will need some coaching on the art of projecting their voices. The following are some very simple techniques:

- Speak from the gut level rather than the throat. If you try to speak loudly but tighten your throat, you'll wear your voice out quickly.
- Use focusing images. When you are onstage, pick a spot on the farthest back wall of the theater and practice speaking to it. Practice sending your voice to points you've chosen that are different distances from you without whispering or yelling: your toes, the chair three feet away, the wall, the room next door, the field outside the building. During performances, even if you are speaking to someone right next to you, keep the thought that you are, at the same time, speaking to the back wall.

- Ask someone to sit or stand as far away from the stage as possible and give you feedback while you say your lines. Do this often enough that you have a sense of how loud you sound to yourself when you are speaking loud enough to be heard.

- Actors always warm up their voices before a performance. Some do singing exercises, some do tongue twisters, some focus on breathing and breath control. For student groups, you can lead some tongue twisters to practice enunciation and to think about the meaning of what you are saying; when you don't keep the meaning in mind, you start conflating the words and goofing up.

- Another simple warm up is to start to pay attention to your breathing— breathe deeply and regularly. After a moment, begin humming and let the vibration from the humming relax your throat. Then open your mouth so that the hum becomes an open-throated drone sound. Again, let the vibrations from your voice relax your throat muscles. Close your lips again to return to a humming sound, then soften that sound until you've faded it out and are simply breathing again.

Bells, Whistles, and Models

Slides. Slides can be projected as a backdrop to enhance a Readers' Theater presentation or suggest the setting for a dramatic scene. You may find slides ready-made and available from museums, but often what you'll find is a photograph. I have had some success making slides from book illustrations or photographs by reducing the images on a high-quality photocopy machine until they are approximately 1"-by-1", then running them on transparency film, cutting them out, and mounting them in slide holders. It's a funky way to do it but fairly inexpensive. Remember to observe copyright laws if you are using images that are protected by copyright. I've found that museums, newspapers, and individual artists are generally willing to give permission in exchange for a thank you in the program.

Songs. There are a number of websites that list lyrics for songs, if you know the title of the song you're looking for. My favorite search engine is Google. Try entering the song title in quotes; if that doesn't lead you directly to something useful, you can enter "song lyrics" as a search term and dig a little deeper. There are so many different websites, with different kinds of lyrics that it would be hard to select just one or two to list here. As far as print resources go, for traditional folk song and popular folk rock lyrics, you can't beat *Rise Up Singing: The Group Singing Songbook* edited by Peter Blood, with an Introduction by Pete Seeger and illustrations by Kore L. McWhirter

(1992). You won't find the tunes in this book, just the lyrics, but you will find references to the recorded versions.

For collections of historical folk music, check out the Smithsonian's Folkways catalogue; you can find a link to it at *www.folkways.si.edu/*. In addition to being able to search by title or by artist, collections are categorized by genre; country; and, in some cases, themes, such as World History and Politics. It probably goes without saying that your students will be, collectively, experts on the current popular music that might find a place in a production.

Samples and Guides. A website maintained by the Smith Research Center at Indiana University *(www.indiana.edu/~eric_rec/ieo/bibs/rdr-thea.html)* provides a number of links to sites about Readers' Theater in elementary and secondary schools, including sample scripts and an ERIC bibliography.

Shakespeare's Stage Theory

"All the world's a stage," William Shakespeare told us, but he went on to characterize one of those stages as "the whining schoolboy creeping like snail unwillingly to school." So it appears that the problem of engaging students in education is not nearly as new as some public school critics would have us think. Be that as it may, giving students opportunities to learn through creating drama is one way, in these times of drastic change, to get them to pick up their cues. Rather than creeping like snails to school, you may find them eager to come and to participate. What better way is there to prepare them for dealing with their future than through experiencing themselves as critical evaluators of historical information and creative conveyors of their own visions?

Let's help students realize the parts they need to play on the world stage by knowing how to think critically, how to inform themselves, how to interpret information, how to connect past to present to future, and how to express themselves effectively. Let's help them make the best possible history.

Resources

Oral History Websites

www.dickinson.edu/oha—Oral History Association
www.geocities.com/aohelanman—Association of Oral History Educators

Books

Blood, Peter (ed.). 1992. *Rise Up Singing: The Group Singing Songbook.* Milwauke, WI: Hal Leonard.
Lanmah, Barry, and George Mehavvy. 1988. *Oral History in the Secondary School Classroom.* Carisle, PA: Oral History Association.
Ritchie, Donald. 1995. *Doing Oral History.* Upper Saddle River, NJ: Prentice Hall.

Selwyn, Douglas. 1993. *Living History in the Classroom.* Tucson, AZ: Zephyr.
Sommer, Barbara, and Mary Kay Quinlan. 2002. *The Oral History Manual.* Walnut Creek, CA: Alta Mira Press.
Wood, Linda P. 2001. *Oral History Projects in Your Classroom.* Carlisle, PA: Oral History Association.

Artists-in-Residence

For assistance in locating a theater artist-in-residence, contact your state, county, and/or local arts commissions. Many of them maintain rosters of artists who have experience working with school-age populations; some commissions may also have grants available. Check out any local theater companies too.

If you are in a city large enough to support one or more professional theater companies, call them to see if they have educational outreach programs. There may be a match between what you need and what they offer. If the theaters near you are semiprofessional or community-based, they may or may not have outreach programs. If not, they may still be able to put you in touch with theater artists who would like to work with school-age groups.

Don't overlook families. You never know until you ask whether there are people with BA or MFA degrees in drama among your students' parents, guardians, siblings, and/or grandparents. This could be just the project for someone who would like to keep her or his toes in theatrical waters but doesn't have the time and/or opportunity to pursue a full-time career.

Glossary

Stage Directions. When an actor moves around on the stage, directions are described from the actor's point of view. *Stage-center* is, of course, the center of the stage. *Stage-right* is to the actor's right as she views the audience; *stage-left* is to the actor's left. When an actor moves away from the audience, toward the back of the stage area, he is moving *upstage.* When he moves toward the audience, nearer the edge of the stage, he is moving *downstage.* All movement can be directed using a combination of these terms. In scripts, the possibilities are generally abbreviated—SC for stage center, USL for upstage left, XDSR for cross downstage right, and so on.

Upstaging. Basically this means interfering with the focus that someone else rightly deserves at a particular moment in a play. It derives from the fact that if you stand upstage of another actor, it forces her to turn her back to the audience in order to look at you. It's a very rude thing to do to a fellow performer. Few actors do it on purpose, but it can happen inadvertently. Inexperienced actors often upstage themselves by turning their backs to the audience even when they have monologues. You can help students avoid upstaging each other by asking them to always stand more or less on the same parallel as any other actor if they are in dialogue with that actor. Also remind them to make sure their feet always describe an arc that includes more than half of the audience. Another way to think of it: If they can't see the audience, the audience can't see them.

Places. The positions the actors take just before a scene begins are known as *places.* Places at the beginning of the show means the actors are offstage just before the houselights go down or onstage just before the curtain rises. When you call "Places, please," your actors should immediately go to wherever they should be. "Places for the top of the show" means they go to wherever they are to be when the show starts. "Places for Scene 2" means they take up whatever positions they are to be in at the very beginning of Scene 2. Teaching students to respond quickly to the "places" call is essential; otherwise, you'll waste valuable time rounding them up in less efficient ways.

Cue. A *cue* is whatever signals actors or stage technicians to say their next line or perform their next action. The cue for taking places on the stage at the beginning of the show is usually a blackout or a spoken cue from the stage manager. In dialogue, the cue is generally the last word spoken by the other actor. "Pick up your cues," an oft-heard note from directors, means to respond more quickly to whatever the cues are. You can practice this skill, and have a lot of fun, by having a *cue rehearsal*—the actors practice beginning their lines as soon as they hear the next-to-last word spoken prior, and then speaking double-time. A *cue-to-cue* rehearsal is a technical rehearsal in which only the transitions involving light and sound cues are rehearsed.

On-book and Off-book. When actors memorize their lines, they are said to be *off-book.* When they are first off-book, they often forget lines. In these cases, it is helpful to have one of the crew members *on-book* as a prompter. This means they follow along in the script, and when the actor forgets a line, they call it out loudly and neutrally so that the actor can remember and go on. The convention is for the actor who has forgotten a line to call "Line!" and the prompter to respond with the first part of the line. Once you are in final rehearsals, you may want to tell your actors that you want them to struggle through memory lapses instead of calling for lines so that they practice another important skill, *covering.* If they've had sufficient rehearsal time, and know their characters and the basic meaning/action of the scene they're playing, they'll be able to *cover* for themselves and each other by paraphrasing. If they do it well, no one, including you, will even know it happened.